Russell Sturgis, J. W. Root and others

Homes in City and Country

Russell Sturgis, J. W. Root and others

Homes in City and Country

ISBN/EAN: 9783744790710

Printed in Europe, USA, Canada, Australia, Japan

Cover: Foto ©Suzi / pixelio.de

More available books at **www.hansebooks.com**

COUNTRY PLACE OF SEVEN ACRES OVERLOOKING THE HUDSON.

HOMES IN CITY
AND COUNTRY

BY

RUSSELL STURGIS   DONALD G. MITCHELL
JOHN W. ROOT   SAMUEL PARSONS, Jr.
BRUCE PRICE   W. A. LINN

WITH ONE HUNDRED ILLUSTRATIONS

NEW YORK
CHARLES SCRIBNER'S SONS
1893

TROW DIRECTORY
PRINTING AND BOOKBINDING COMPANY
NEW YORK

CONTENTS

	PAGE
THE CITY HOUSE IN THE EAST AND SOUTH, . . .	1
BY RUSSELL STURGIS.	
THE CITY HOUSE IN THE WEST, ...	35
BY JOHN W. ROOT.	
THE SUBURBAN HOUSE, ...	70
BY BRUCE PRICE.	
THE COUNTRY HOUSE, ...	99
BY DONALD G. MITCHELL.	
SMALL COUNTRY PLACES, ...	137
BY SAMUEL PARSONS, Jr.	
BUILDING AND LOAN ASSOCIATIONS, ...	160
BY W. A. LINN.	

LIST OF ILLUSTRATIONS

FULL-PAGE ILLUSTRATIONS

	PAGE
COUNTRY PLACE OF SEVEN ACRES OVERLOOKING THE HUDSON,	*Frontispiece*
THE SEARS HOUSES, NOW THE SOMERSET CLUB, EXEMPLIFYING THE MORE SUMPTUOUS BOSTON HOUSE OF 1840 AND LATER,	11
HOUSE OF FIRE-CLAY BRICKS IN PRAIRIE AVENUE, CHICAGO, ILL.,	49
ROMAN BRICK HOUSE IN NORTH STATE STREET, CHICAGO, ILL.,	57
HOUSE IN DENVER, COL.,	65
THE OSBORN HOUSE AT MAMARONECK, N. Y.,	71
SHINGLE HOUSE AT CAMBRIDGE, MASS., RICHARDSON, ARCHITECT,	85
THE NEWCOMBE HOUSE AT ELBERON, N. J., MCKIM, ARCHITECT,	91
AN ARTISTIC COTTAGE AT SHORT HILLS, N. J.,	95
LINKLAEN HOUSE (EIGHTEENTH CENTURY) CAZENOVIA, N. Y.,	111
WADSWORTH HOMESTEAD IN THE GENESEE VALLEY, WESTERN NEW YORK,	119
HYDE HALL, COOPERSTOWN, N. Y.,	123
HOUSE OF EDWARD LIVINGSTON, LENOX, MASS.,	127
HOUSE OF LYMAN JOSEPHS, NEWPORT, R. I.,	133
A COUNTRY PLACE OF SEVEN ACRES, WITH POND, IN THE MIDST OF OPEN COUNTRY,	149

ILLUSTRATIONS IN THE TEXT

	PAGE
OLD BRICK HOUSES ON WASHINGTON SQUARE, NORTH, NEW YORK,	4
OLD TYPE OF HOUSE IN BEACH STREET, BOSTON,	8
REAR VIEW OF HOUSES AT EIGHTH AND SPRUCE STREETS, PHILADELPHIA,	13
GROUP OF HOUSES AT THIRD AND LOCUST STREETS, PHILADELPHIA; BUILT ABOUT 1810,	14
SOUTHERN HOUSE WITH VERANDAS IN CHARLESTON, S. C.,	15
WIDE HOUSE IN WASHINGTON PLACE, NEW YORK,	17
BRICK HOUSE, CORNER OF EAST SIXTY-EIGHTH STREET AND PARK AVENUE, NEW YORK; BUILT ABOUT 1880,	21
MODERN YELLOW BRICK HOUSE IN EAST THIRTY-THIRD STREET, NEW YORK,	26
HOUSE IN EAST FORTY-NINTH STREET, NEW YORK,	27
OLD NEW YORK HOUSES, NOW THE COLONNADE HOTEL, LAFAYETTE PLACE, NEW YORK,	28
CORNER HOUSE IN WEST END AVENUE, NEW YORK,	31
OLD HOUSE IN CINCINNATI, O.,	41
BRICK AND TERRA-COTTA HOUSE ON DEARBORN AVENUE, CHICAGO, ILL.,	53
REDDISH-BROWN SANDSTONE HOUSE ON DEARBORN AVENUE, CHICAGO, ILL.,	55
HOUSE OF ROUGH-FACED BRICK IN BELLEVUE PLACE, CHICAGO, ILL.,	59
A PICTURESQUE HOUSE IN ST. LOUIS, MO.,	60
WOODEN HOUSE IN MILWAUKEE, WIS., WITH STUCCO-FRIEZE,	61
HOUSE IN MINNEAPOLIS, MINN.,	68
TERRACED HOUSE AT TACOMA, WASH.,	79
SUBURBAN HOUSE OF MODERATE PRETENSIONS AT TUXEDO, N. Y.,	80
SHINGLE-WORK HOUSE AT MORRISTOWN, N. J.,	81
HOUSE AT CUMBERLAND, MD.; BUILT FIFTY YEARS AGO,	82
COTTAGE AT NEWPORT, R. I.,	83
HOUSE AT KENWOOD, ILL.,	87

LIST OF ILLUSTRATIONS

	PAGE
SUBURBAN HOUSE AT EVANSTON, ILL.,	88
HOUSE AT CINCINNATI, O.,	89
ENGLISH SUBURBAN HOUSE,	94
ROCK HALL, NEAR ROCKAWAY, LONG ISLAND,	101
EXAMPLE OF OLD HOUSE IN INTERIOR OF CONNECTICUT,	102
RHODE ISLAND AND CONNECTICUT SHORE HOUSE,	103
SPECIMEN OF EARLY DUTCH ARCHITECTURE, LONG ISLAND, N. Y.,	104
RESIDENCE OF JOSEPH HOPKINS SMITH, FALMOUTH, ME.,	105
CHARACTERISTIC NEW ENGLAND HOUSE, ESPECIALLY IN TOWNS ALONG THE CONNECTICUT RIVER,	106
OLD HOUSE OF PETER AVERY, PEQUONNOC, CONN.; BUILT IN 1656,	107
FAIRBANKS HOUSE AT DEDHAM, MASS.; BUILT IN 1636,	108
JOHNSON HALL, JOHNSTOWN, N. Y.; BUILT IN 1764 BY SIR WILLIAM JOHNSON,	109
STRATFORD HOUSE, WESTMORELAND COUNTY, VA.,	115
MANTEL IN THE WISTER HOUSE, GERMANTOWN, PA.,	116
CHEW HOUSE, GERMANTOWN, PA.,	117
STAIRCASE IN WADSWORTH HOUSE, GENESEO,	121
LODGE GATE, HYDE HALL,	125
MCALPIN HOUSE, SING SING, N. Y.,	130
COUNTRY PLACE OF SIX ACRES ON THE EAST RIVER, NEAR NEW YORK,	146
A PLACE OF ABOUT SEVEN ACRES IN A NEW JERSEY HILL TOWN,	153
GROUNDS OF A HOUSE AT A SUMMER WATERING PLACE,	156
RURAL TREATMENT OF A PLACE OF TWO LOTS IN A CITY,	158
A BUILDING AND LOAN ASSOCIATION RECEIVING MONTHLY DUES,	187
HOUSE OF A CARPENTER AT WOLLASTON, MASS.; COST $1,800,	189
ROW OF HOUSES IN READING, PA.; BUILT BY BUILDING AND LOAN ASSOCIATIONS,	192
HOUSE OF A CLERK IN PITTSBURG, PA.; COST ABOUT $2,200,	194

LIST OF ILLUSTRATIONS

	PAGE
HOUSE OF A WESTERN UNION TELEGRAPH SUPERINTENDENT AT MOUNT VERNON, N. Y.; COST $2,200, EXCLUSIVE OF GROUND,	197
HOUSE IN SIXTY-SEVENTH STREET, BAY RIDGE, L. I.; COST $2,500,	198
"THEN AND NOW." FOUR ROOMS RENTED IN THE UPPER FLOOR OF THIS BUILDING AT $9 PER MONTH,	200
HOUSE BUILT AND OCCUPIED BY THE SAME MAN IN HACKENSACK, N. J.; COST $1,050; MONTHLY PAYMENT, $11.50,	200
HOUSE OF A WHOLESALE DRY-GOODS MERCHANT AT BAYONNE, N. J.,	202
HALL BUILT BY THE COLUMBIA ASSOCIATION, JERSEY CITY; COST, WITH LOT, $4,730,	203
HOUSE OF A YOUNG BUSINESS MAN IN ROCHESTER, N. Y.; BUILT ON A WEEKLY PAYMENT OF $7.25, FOR A PERIOD OF ABOUT NINE YEARS,	205
HOUSE OF A TAILOR IN ST. PAUL, MINN.; COST $1,860,	206
HOUSE OF A BUILDING AND LOAN ASSOCIATION SECRETARY IN ST. LOUIS; COST, WITHOUT LOT, $7,000,	208
HOUSE OF A CINCINNATI BOOKKEEPER; COST, WITH LOT, $2,400,	209
HOUSE OF A BOOKKEEPER AT BERKELEY, A SUBURB OF SAN FRANCISCO, CAL.; COST $2,000,	210
HOUSE OF A GOVERNMENT CLERK IN WASHINGTON, D. C.; COST $4,000,	211
HOUSE OF A PRESSMAN IN NEW ORLEANS; COST, WITH LOT, $4,227,	213

HOMES IN CITY AND COUNTRY

THE CITY HOUSE IN THE EAST AND SOUTH

By RUSSELL STURGIS

IN this chapter a city house is assumed to be one which forms part of a thickly built neighborhood. The city house, according to this standard, occupies a lot which it almost entirely fills. It is either enclosed on both sides, so as to have its windows in the two narrow faces only, or else, if a corner house, it has the street on two sides of it, and another house set close against it on one side. Houses which are freer in this respect, and have windows on all four sides, and those which have, moreover, some ground about them, which circumstance will usually modify their plan, come under the head of suburban houses, and will be considered at another time.

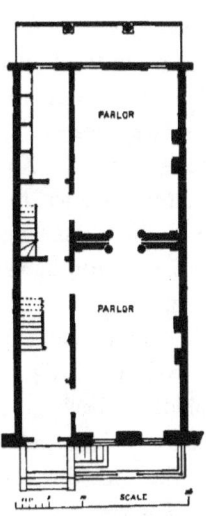

Plan 1.—A Washington Square House, New York, about 1830.

The very simple New York house of 1830 and the years following, and the more stately houses of the same epoch were alike planned nearly as in Plan 1. The mansion of Washington Square and the six-thousand-dollar house of an out-of-the-way street differ merely in dimensions, and in such minor features as the presence or absence of the columns which seem to reinforce the partition between the parlors, and the similar architectural adornments of the principal entrance.

The stoop * contained not less than eight risers in addition to the door-sill; that is to say, the visitor had to mount at least nine steps from the sidewalk to reach the parlor floor; very often there were eleven or twelve steps in all. Indeed, one gentleman of the old school, who, in 1870, was building a house into which he wished to incorporate his reminiscences of the early time, insisted on a total height of seven feet seven inches for his stoop, or thirteen risers of seven inches each, which he thought was the normal height and arrangement of a New York stoop. In houses of 1830, both the larger and the smaller, the front basement room was expected to be used as a dining-room. So much of the common London house plan was retained, with, however, this important difference—that instead of entering the house on the dining-room floor, and going upstairs to the drawing-rooms, you entered the house on the drawing-room floor, and were obliged to go downstairs to the dining-room. The kitchen occupied the back part of the basement story, and between the kitchen and the dining-room were closets and pantries, with sometimes a trap in the wall through which dishes could be passed, and sometimes a free doorway. The back yard was not, as has been the later custom, dug out to the level of six or eight inches below the kitchen floor, but remained at the original level, and an area, that is, a sunken enclosure with retaining walls and a few rough stone steps, was made for access to the kitchen. In the second story there was the well-known arrangement of a large bedroom in front with two windows, and a small one adjoining it; the same arrangement in the rear, and the space between the two large bedrooms occupied by closets, called in New York, of old, always "pantries."

After the introduction of the Croton water into New York, a bath was put up in the smaller back room, or, as it is generally called now-

---

* This word, of Dutch origin, once unknown outside of New York and its immediate vicinity, but now in use throughout the country, is a desirable addition to the language, for it expresses what no other English word does. It corresponds very closely to the French *perron*.

adays, the back hall-bedroom; and, in houses built after the introduction of Croton water, this was almost uniformly used as the bathroom. The water-supply in these houses was, however, limited to this bathroom and to the kitchen sink. There were no "set" wash-trays, no water-supply for the furnace—for there was no furnace, at least of the modern sort—no permanent basins in the bedrooms, no sinks or other conveniences to which water was supplied; furthermore, there was no dumb-waiter connecting the kitchen floor and the parlor floor, because it was not expected that the family would eat anywhere except in the front basement room. Access to the roof was by means of a movable ladder. The cellar was paved with cobble-stones, and had no fittings beyond a few shelves and one or two "hanging shelves," which were light platforms, hung by strips of wood nailed to the beams overhead; but at least every house had a cellar under its whole extent, and this partly made up for the absent garret, which the growing disposition to make what are called flat roofs—that is, roofs with a very slight inclination, and covered, usually, with metal—was beginning to banish. Such a house, if it had two full stories of bedrooms above the parlors, was still called a "two-story house with finished attic," that is to say, the parlor story counted as one, and the second bedroom story was still the attic, whether it was everywhere nine feet or more high in the clear, or whether, as often happened, the slope of the roof cut off the back rooms to a height of six or even five feet at the rear wall. The front was of plain brick, with white marble lintels and stoop in the handsomer houses of Bleecker Street, Washington Place, Washington Square, and the like, or of Connecticut brown stone in Clinton Place, lower Fifth Avenue, Second Avenue, St. Mark's Place, and in other parts of the town. There was extreme simplicity in all the fittings and appointments, with the exception of here and there a costly detail; thus, in many of these houses, the doors of the parlor story, and sometimes of the first bedroom story, were of mahogany or rosewood veneered work, extremely handsome, well-made, and costly, while all the woodwork around them was of

Houses on Washington Square, North, New York.

white pine, simply painted white, and without carving or ornament of applied composition. The tendency of the epoch thirty years earlier for rather elaborate decoration, with plaster, stucco, and the like, in the classical style, and applied freely to cornices and ceilings, had also disappeared, and a severe uniformity had become the rule.

The picture on p. 4 gives the exterior of such a house, taken from one of those now standing on the north side of Washington Square. The only discrepancy between plan and exterior view is that the latter has a more elaborate entrance; the doorway proper more deeply recessed and decorated with wooden columns within the recess, while a marble porch decorates the opening in the house-wall.

In Baltimore and the more Southern cities a very different plan of house, and one more nearly approaching the suburban type, was usual. Plan 2 shows the ground-floor of such a house of the smaller and cheaper sort, and it will be seen that such a plan presupposes lower prices for land and the possibility of using, for an eight-thousand or a ten-thousand dollar house, a larger, or at least a wider, lot than New York allowed to a house of twice the cost. The front building has but one room and the staircase hall in its depth; and this front building is usually three actual stories in height, namely, the ground-story, raised only two or three steps above the sidewalk; the drawing-room story above this, and a third story containing perhaps two bedrooms. The back building contains, above the rooms shown in the plan, at least one story of bedrooms. The back stairs leading from the kitchen communicate with this and with a sort of a garret above. There is no water-supply to the house except a pump at the end of the yard, which pump, however, was replaced by a hydrant when water from an aqueduct was to be had.

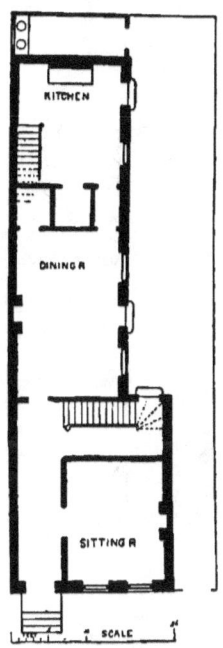

Plan 2.—Ground Plan of a Southern House.

Plan 3 shows a modification of this plan in the direction of greater elegance and cost. The plan is as noticeable for convenience and pleasantness, as, in its smaller way, is Plan 2. The little passage leading to the side door would seem to separate the dining-room from the parlors enough and not too much.

The superiority of these plans over the New York one, in all that goes to make up the comfort of domestic life, is obvious; but their merits are directly traceable to the low price of land. The unfortunate step taken long ago by our now-forgotten predecessors of placing New York City on this narrow island of Manhattan was felt in its fatal influence on the comfort of our homes before New York contained a quarter of a million of inhabitants.

The Boston type of house, Plans 4 and 5, seems to indicate a still greater scarcity of land than existed in New York, in which latter city the streets at least were tolerably wide and allowed of the usual exterior appliances — stoops, areas, and courtyards, to use the most familiar terms. Boston, indeed, was a very crowded place before the building up of Back Bay was begun. The curious arrangement of the entrance flight of steps within the wall of the house was as characteristic a

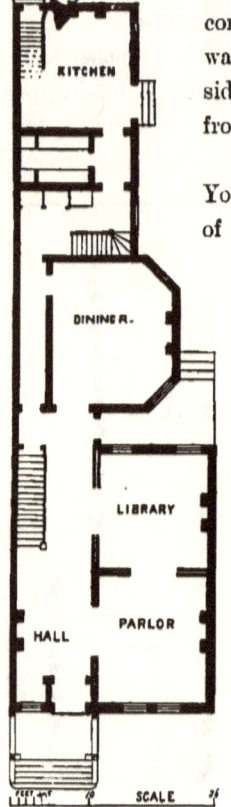

Plan 3.—Ground Floor of a House in Richmond, Va.

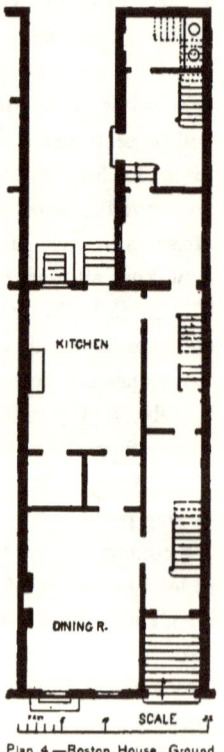

Plan 4.—Boston House, Ground Floor.

feature of Boston streets as any that could be named. Plan 4 shows the lowest story, raised five or six steps above the sidewalk. The front room was nearly always arranged for a dining-room, and so used; the back room was the kitchen, and beneath this story there was nothing but the cellar, raised half above the ground, like a New York basement story, and including the curious "archway," by means of which access was had to the kitchen by the tradesmen supplying the family. The butcher-boy, ringing at the archway bell, plunged down a steep flight of steps when the door was opened, passed through a passage-way partitioned off from the cellar, mounted a second flight of steps to the back yard, and so found himself opposite the kitchen door. It was, indeed, the Baltimore or Philadelphia alley adapted to a small lot by being put under the house instead of beside it; and there were Boston houses which retained the alley on the street level, and were carried over it and so made wider in the upper stories. Plan 5 shows the drawing-room floor of the same Boston house; and, as the room back of the staircase was often arranged for a china-closet, it would seem that the Boston family used often to dine in the back parlor. There was no dumb-waiter, to be

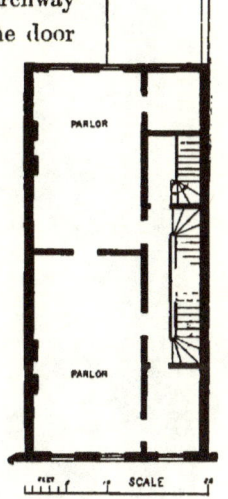

Plan 5.—Boston House, Second Floor.

sure, but Boston always was inclined to take after London, and to this day a waiting-maid in a London house brings all the dishes for the table up at least one flight of stairs to the dining-room, an arrangement which a New York maid or man would consider quite out of the question. There was no plumbing and no water-supply in such a house except in the kitchen, no dumb-waiter, no furnace. When the Cochituate water was brought into the city a bath-room was perhaps fitted up in the ground-floor extension, or more rarely in the third

Old Type of House in Beach Street, Boston.

story. The cost of such a house was about the same as that of a New York house of the same size, but the Boston lot was not usually of the full depth of a hundred feet. In view of the small size of the back yard, the "wash" was dried on the roof of the one-story extension, and the frames and racks adapted to this purpose were a characteristic feature of the interior of an old Boston block.

The annexed picture is a front view of just such a house, except that it is reversed from the plan, and has the entrance on the left. The steps that lead up to the front door might be of wood, as they were partially protected from the weather, and they were so except in rather costly houses.

It was noticeable that in these houses there was no projection of any sort beyond the house-wall, nothing belonging to the house which in any way encroached upon the street. Perhaps a scraper for the feet at the main entrance would be the only accessory which invaded the public way, or perhaps the uppermost step of the flight leading to the archway would invade the sidewalk to the width of a foot or somewhat less. The New Yorker walking along the Boston streets had a curious sensation of brushing the walls of the houses with his elbow, and of being within two feet of the people looking out of the windows of the ground floor. Something of the same kind we shall find in Philadelphia. The narrow and crooked streets, lined on both sides with houses like these, gave a singular air of sternness and simplicity to the town, and caused to a certain extent what was called the English look of Boston.

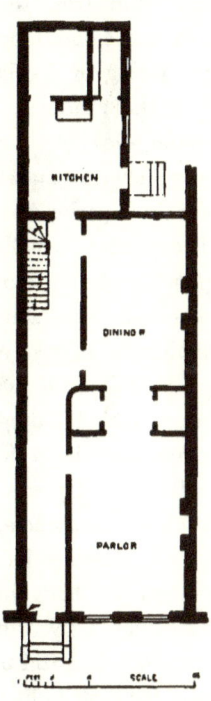

Plan 6.—Ground Floor of a Philadelphia House.

In the three typical houses we have been considering, it was always assumed that the dining-room would be on the floor below that occupied by the drawing-room or rooms; but in Philadelphia a type of house was in use from an early time which put all the living-rooms on one floor, and very nearly on the level of the street. It is curious to see this retention of an eminently out-of-town feature in so thickly built a city. Plan 6 gives us the ground floor of such a house as this. The wealthy Quaker merchants of Philadelphia may be said to have brought this kind of house to as great perfection as the plan allows. Their fittings and decorations were of the most simple character, so far as the variety of form and color is concerned, but the workmanship was excellent, and there was no rejection of such worldly features as expensive wall-paper with gold patterns on a gray ground, and doors and mantlepieces of somewhat costly materials. In general, the fittings and appointments were at least as good as those of Boston and New York. As regards the plan, it must not be forgotten that the Philadelphia house communicated with a back alley running through the block, from which there was a gateway through the back wall of the yard and thence to the kitchen. In front, therefore, on the street, there needed to be but one entrance, and this was raised not more than five risers from the sidewalk. There was no front area, of course, and the smooth brick sidewalk was carried unbroken to the marble facing of the basement story, so that any passer-by could look in at the windows. The front parlor was made as wide as the house would allow, leaving only about five feet or thereabout for the passageway; but the staircase hall in the rear was necessarily wider, so that the back parlor was two feet or three feet narrower than the front. The staircase usually went up in double flights with platforms. In this plan the dining-room is supposed to be the back parlor, and this arrangement was facilitated by the closets between the two parlors, convenient in themselves and forming a lobby or short passage with two pairs of doors if desired. Houses somewhat more expensive have a larger back building than is sufficient for the kitchen and its appurtenances, and have the dining-room itself in that **L**. No service room or butler's pantry was obtainable on the smaller plan, but access to the kitchen was sufficiently convenient, while at the same time there was no unnecessary discomfort caused by its too great vicinity. The upper stories had this peculiarity, that the staircase hall was always well-lighted by windows on the platforms of the staircase; for the back building did not extend above the first story. The inhabitants paid for their light staircase and hall by giving up one of the possible hall-bedrooms on each floor. Houses like this, and in desirable neighborhoods too, would rent for from $600 to $800 at a time when in New York absolutely nothing of the sort was known; when, even as now, one had to go to South Brooklyn or to Harlem for a six-hundred-

The Sears Houses, now the Somerset Club, exemplifying the more sumptuous Boston House of 1840 and later. (The "archway" is retained in the passage leading from the doorway in the Terrace Wall.)

dollar house and nearly as far for an eight-hundred-dollar one. Philadelphia as well as Baltimore had the advantage of plenty of land to spread over. It used this great advantage in a way not decorative or poetical assuredly, but in the most economical fashion, so as to make possible thousands of comfortable and sufficient private houses.

Rear View of Houses at Eighth and Spruce Streets, Philadelphia.

The picture above shows the exterior, not indeed of just such a house as we have been describing, but of the corner house of a block of just such houses. The entrance being on the side street, around the corner, changes the arrangement of the principal rooms, and there is a much larger area enclosed from the street than we had assumed to be customary; but the back building containing the kitchen, the red brick and white marble, and above all the display of white-painted solid shutters at all the windows, above and below, are as characteristic as possible. These Philadelphia houses are so fasci-

Group of Houses at Third and Locust Streets, Philadelphia; built about 1810.

nating in their simplicity and homeliness, that it seems worth while to give in the picture above a row of smaller ones, older perhaps than the types we have been considering, perhaps of about 1810, adorned with a little colored brick-work, and more picturesque than a later taste allowed.

The types followed in the more Southern cities vary too much for us to study them in detail. Thus, in New Orleans, the building of the larger houses around courts, or with large paved yards between the house and the street, made the type of smaller houses very uncertain. Each builder of a small house tried to secure some of the features of the larger ones, and the result was endless variety. In Savannah the house of the better class was apt to have the parlors, dining-room, etc., in a long suite, with windows opening on a garden which stretched the whole length of the house. In Charleston the houses were more like those in Northern cities, except the mansions of considerable size; these had "galleries," or verandas, sometimes two stories of them, as in the picture below, and resembled suburban rather than city houses. It is hard to establish a type for the smaller houses of the

House in Charleston, S. C.

Southern cities. It is quite probable that there was not quite so uniform a gradation between the humblest and the more elegant houses as in the North.

Wealthier families at the North, as well as at the South, enjoyed double houses, that is to say, houses with rooms on both sides of the entrance hall, occupying for the purpose lots of ground from thirty-seven to fifty feet in width. It is remarkable, however, that very few such houses were built in New York, as compared with the much greater number in Baltimore and Philadelphia, and even in crowded Boston. Mr. Bristed, in his "Upper Ten Thousand," the letters composing which work were contributed to *Frazer's Magazine* about 1845, puts his typical New York grandee into a house three rooms deep and twenty-seven feet wide, and explains that this house occupied a corner lot, and thus had the advantage of windows in the second room of the three. Indeed, anyone who knew New York about 1845, will remember how unusual was the house with four or five windows in one story of its front. Still, such houses were known. The picture on page 17 shows one that must have been a delightful residence; it is now no longer a private dwelling. The Boston double house was apt to be of the type shown in Plan 7. The lot is about forty feet wide. The two large parlors are in themselves almost exactly reproductions of the two parlors of the narrower houses that we have been considering; but, as half of the width of the lot is allowed them, they are broader, and with the width goes generally greater length. The plan, as it is given here, is a Boston plan, but the New York house of the same character was very like it, except that the rounded front of the parlor would be absent; for these "swell fronts" were essentially a Boston peculiarity, and but two or three groups of them existed in New York. A similar house was built on a narrower lot, thirty-two feet wide or thereabouts, with this change, namely, that the dining-room, instead of slipping past the back parlor in the direction of the length of the house, so as to allow of a door in the longi-

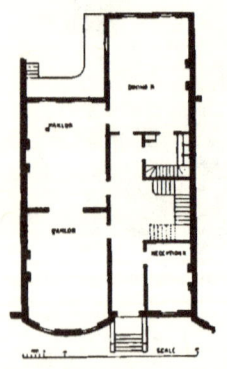

Plan 7.—Ground Floor, Boston Double-house.

THE CITY HOUSE IN THE EAST AND SOUTH 17

House in Washington Place, New York.

tudinal partition, as in Plan 7, was slipped past the back parlor the other way, or transversely, so that the door leading from the back parlor to the dining-room would be in the rear wall of the latter, and the back parlor would have but one window.

In this plan, the stoop, with entrance directly to the principal floor, was still maintained. With this exception, it is curious how like the plan is to a well-known English one. Plan 8 represents a house to which many an American has gone to see the beautiful works of art which it contained —a simple house in a quarter of London very fashionable forty years ago, and still respectable, with a venerable air of bygone magnificence. Here, as in pretty much all London houses, the entrance is on what we should call the basement floor, and on the same floor as the dining-room. The principal story is, therefore, left free from the annoyance of the entrance from the street, and consists of a series of drawing-rooms and sitting-rooms. The plan differs from that of other London houses of the same epoch, and of some dignity, chiefly in the great prolongation of the L or extension, so as to make a double picture-gallery of considerable size, lighted from the roof as well as from the side wall. Ordinarily, such a house had an extension of not more than fifteen feet from the rear wall of the main building, and a morning-room or sitting-room of moderate size occupied the whole of this. The immense superiority, for all purposes of elegant social life, of this plan over the Boston one is obvious. The only advantage which the Boston plan has is that of having the dining-room on the same floor as the sitting-room and drawing-room, so that dinner guests assembling in any of these rooms can go to the dining-room, and can, later, pass from the dining-room to the drawing-room without going up and down stairs. This advantage is perhaps fully counterbalanced by the avoidance of the neighborhood of the dining-room with its odors, so unwelcome after the dinner is over. In a city house

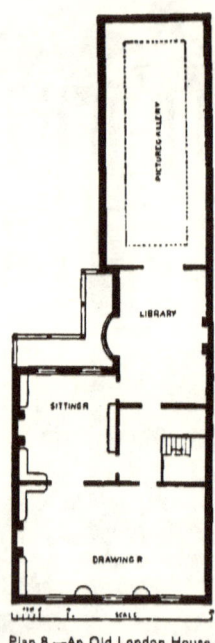

Plan 8.—An Old London House.

there is hardly room for the dining-room on the same floor with the drawing-room, without this annoyance; and in all other respects the London plan has the clear advantage, the rooms for family life and for entertainment being alike free from the double annoyance of the doorway to the street with its passage or entry cutting across the sequence of the apartments, and of the dining-room with its pantries and other appurtenances. There is, indeed, but one good reason for the adoption of the " high-stoop " plan, and that is the lack, in this country, of fairly well-trained servants. The lady of the house receiving in London is supposed to ring for a servant to show her guest to the outer door, to open it and close it again. In planning the American house, it is assumed that she will not have servants enough, or well-trained enough, to allow of such a manner of speeding her parting guest; she is supposed to be left to her own resources, and to be more able to see that her guests get out of the house in safety if she is herself in the room immediately adjoining the entrance. No other reason has ever been suggested, so far as the author knows, for the solecism, almost universal in America now, of having the principal rooms for entertainment and family life as close as possible to the street door. It is, in fact, a country plan or a suburban plan, adapted badly enough to city uses. It dates from a time when the door-bell did not ring much more often in a city house than the knocker sounded in a country house; from a time when there was practically no service, and when, the door standing open in pleasant weather, the visitor or messenger or tradesman announced his presence as best he could, by rapping at the open door, or by hemming or coughing in the front hall; when, during the hours of an evening entertainment, no interruption was to be expected, and when morning or afternoon visiting was so far informal and a matter of free intercourse between neighbors, that there was little call for further ceremony than the good-by at the door.

Such, then, were the houses in which our fathers lived when they were obliged to confine their habitations to city lots. They may be taken as dating from 1830, and any inquiry that we have to make into the later development of the American city plans will begin with 1850, leaving between these two dates a space of time great enough to form a visible boundary between the plans of the old time and the plans of the new time. In dealing with modern plans, we have to consider a much more self-conscious and deliberate epoch than that which went before. As writers of the history of the grander forms of architecture draw a sharp line between all the styles existing previous to the classic revival of the fifteenth century and those that have succeeded it, that line separating the unconscious and, so to speak, aboriginal styles of architecture from the deliberately worked-up and thought-out styles that we know as modern, so, in dealing with these American house plans, we must separate rather sharply the simple plans of our ancestors from the modern ones, supposed to be the deliberately worked-out conceptions of their authors.

Let us hasten to say that this last theory is not yet completely realized. New York is held back by a half-and-half adoption of the modern idea. Boston is wiser or more fortunate in this, that the modern idea is more faithfully followed up. In Boston, the man of some means, who wishes to have a house, employs an architect whom he considers the most intelligent or the most agreeable, and builds his house; in New York, the man, even of wealth, goes with his wife to look at ready-made houses, and accepts, buys, and pays for the one which is the least objectionable. In other words, the Boston man has his clothes carefully made for him by a tailor whom he thinks skilful: the New York man buys his clothes ready-made. Oddly enough, this comparison, if taken literally, is the reverse of true; for the New York man is notoriously the most carefully dressed man on the continent, and has, as Mark Twain says, "a godless grace and snap and style" about himself and his dress which the people of other communities find it impossible to reproduce; but in building—except in the obviously exceptional case of palaces—elegance, comfort, and a careful adaptation of means to an end, are less studied in

Brick House, corner of East Sixty-eighth Street and Park Avenue, New York, built about 1880.
(A good example of appropriate architectural effect produced without sculptured ornament or expensive stone-cutting.)

New York than in any other community which can in any respect be compared with it.

The modern New York house in its original state is, of course, the simple house, Plan 1, with the addition of a back room and a vestibule. The back room was called the "third room," the "tea-room," and often the "extension." Originally this room formed really a one-story extension, and was most commonly built as an after-thought and an addition to the house as at first planned. The next step was to include such a room as this in the house as originally conceived. Plan 9 shows this change and shows also the step that immediately and inevitably followed, namely, the abandonment of the division wall between the two parlors, and the substitution for it of a screen of columns. One great reason for this change was the disagreeable effect of a room with no windows. By doing away with the wall between the front and the back parlor, the two parlors became one room, and there was no longer a room without a window; but an obvious improvement upon this was to do away with the screen of columns also, and to substitute either a transom, or a slightly indicated arch, across the long and narrow parlor; which arch or transom, in its turn, disappeared, and the whole space was treated as a single room, having probably a single fireplace in the middle of the wall, and perhaps a single doorway from the entry. It is hardly necessary to show these different steps in separate cuts. In all of them the back room is prepared for use as a dining-room, and that part of the hall or entry which is enclosed, next adjoining it, is fitted with a dumb-waiter and cupboards, so as to answer for a small service-room, or, as it is called in New York, a butler's pantry.

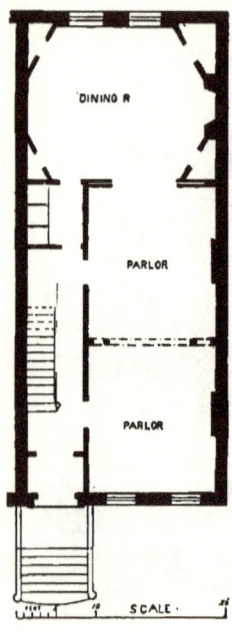

Plan 9.—New York House, 1860, Ground Floor Plan.

The depth of the house thus obtained would have been fifty-seven or fifty-eight feet if the full length of the old parlors had been retained; but it has often happened that the one long parlor which has succeeded them is shortened from forty to thirty-four feet, or even less, so that, with a back room fifteen feet wide, the house, with its walls, is brought within fifty feet. This is a reasonable depth, leaving a satisfactory back yard; and this depth is carried up for the full height of the house. There appeared, contemporaneously with these changes in the main floor, the common addition of a third story of bedrooms, making what would have been called forty years ago a three-story-and-attic house, but which we call to-day, more simply and naturally, a four-story house. These two changes, coming together as they did, raised the price of New York houses considerably, for there were no houses constructed on the older and simple plan, or almost none. To find the seven-thousand dollar or eight-thousand-dollar house of 1850 and later years, one has to take either a house sixteen feet wide or even twelve and a half feet wide, or less, or else go far afield. It has been extremely difficult to get a house for a reasonable price or a reasonable rent in New York, and the reason for that is obvious: space is so much in demand for houses that will bring $20,000, and over, that it is found far more profitable to provide such houses than smaller ones, except, of course, in the forgotten parts of the city, where persons with any pretensions to a claim to polite society do not wish to live.

There was, however, a good deal of sense in this ground-floor plan, and it maintained itself for thirty years as almost the only pattern for houses worth, with the land, from $20,000 to $35,000. The plan of the bedroom floor of such a house was also very sensible and reasonable, when there was not too eager an attempt to get a great many bedrooms, resulting in the use for that purpose of some rooms not properly lighted. For a family not too large for the house no plan is likely to be better than the one shown in Plan 10, where a large bedroom at the front and a large bedroom at the back are at once divided and connected by a passage-way with cupboards on each side, each room having also a separate large closet, in which a water-supply can easily be arranged and often is provided. The two smaller rooms can be used either as two bedrooms, or one of them as a sitting-room, sewing-room, or the like. In plans of this simple kind one of these rooms, and perhaps one on the third bedroom floor, is used for a bathroom, as indeed Plan 10 shows. When the house is somewhat deeper, and the space between the two large bedrooms thereby increased, the bathroom is often put in the middle of the house between the closets which connect the large bedrooms. In this case a light-shaft from the roof gives light and ventilation. These light-shafts have been interfered with by the recent New York building laws, as indeed there was reason, for they are a terrible danger on account of their adaptedness to serve as flues for spreading fire rapidly from floor to floor.

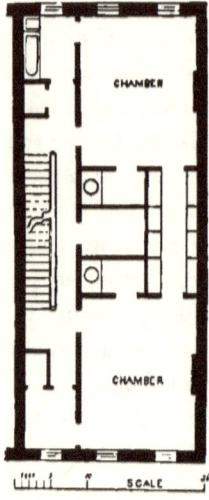

Plan 10.—New York House, 1860, Second Floor.

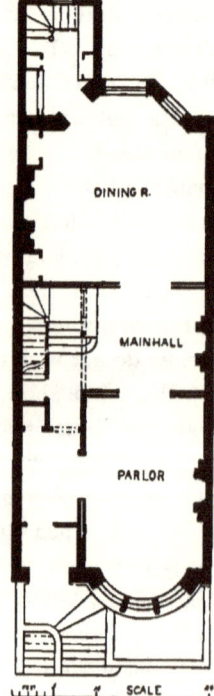

Plan 11.—Modern New York House, West End Avenue.

One of the most approved recent modifications of this arrangement is shown in Plan 11.* The main peculiarity in this is the resolute insistence on something in the way of a hall, which shall replace the long, narrow entrance-way called by that name by former generations. Out of this square hall the staircase to the upper stories must necessarily lead, and the completeness of the screening of this staircase

* House in West End Avenue, designed by Messrs. Berg & Clark.

from the hall, so as to make the access to it partly private from at least a part of the house, is the main point of difference among many different modern houses. In some an architectural screen is arranged, amounting almost to a complete partition, so that, unless doors are left open, the staircase is in an apartment by itself; in others, as in the one before us, this separation is effected by means of an open arcade, or row of columns, with curtains which can be adjusted at pleasure. Whether this plan is agreeable or not in daily use, depends on the habits of the family. It seems to be founded largely upon the idea that a hall and staircase should be handsome and spacious, and that a house that has not a handsome and spacious hall and staircase is an inferior one. This theory cannot be maintained in all cases. It may often be better to reduce the entrance-way and the staircase to the narrowest and humblest dimensions reconcilable with convenience, in order that the rooms actually lived in may be the larger. It is a quite defensible proposition that passage-ways and stairways need only be wide enough to make the moving of furniture into and out of the house practicable, and that every available inch of room should be put into rooms which are capable of being wholly shut off from the passages. The square hall in the middle of the house, as it has been introduced into such New York houses as cost, with the land, from $20,000 to $35,000, is certainly open to the objection that it is not a comfortable or agreeable sitting-room, because too public and because not easily made warm, while, on the

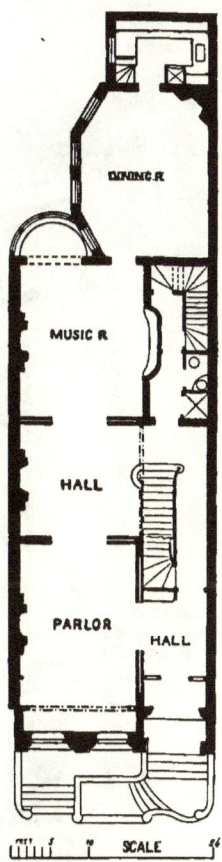

Plan 12.—First Floor of House in Eighty-first Street, New York.

other hand, it is altogether unnecessary as a means of communication between more secluded and more pleasant apartments. It remains to be seen whether the whole scheme will be abandoned, as a temporary "fad," or whether modifications can be introduced into it which will make it a permanent feature of our residences.

Plan 12 shows a house which occupies nearly the whole of its hundred-foot lot.* The arrangements by which the four rooms en suite are made all accessible and convenient, whether used separately or together, are certainly excellent, nor is it easy to see how the ground can be used to better advantage.

Before leaving the consideration of these

House in East Thirty-third Street, New York.

* House in West Eighty-first Street, fronting on Manhattan Square, Messrs. Berg & Clark, architects.

twenty-five-foot and twenty-two-foot houses, standing in the middle of blocks, reference must be made to our illustrations, which give the fronts of such houses as these. Thus, the picture on p. 26 shows a very original and certainly effective façade, executed in light yellow brick, with the entire frame-work and architectural setting of the windows in terra cotta, a few shades darker than the color of the walls. The picture on this page gives an admirable design; one of the most simple and yet effective and spirited fronts which New York can show. The picture on p. 28 shows one section or bay of the well-known row of houses in Lafayette Place; this is of the old and almost forgotten New York, and contrasts with the very recently built exteriors.

There is no doubt that until very much greater familiarity with the possibilities of our narrow fronts has been gained by close and minute study of their decorative treatment by our architects, severe restraint and an almost complete abstinence from elaborate ornament form the only safe course to pursue. Not only architectural sculpture in the strict sense is to be avoided, until it has been much more thoroughly studied

House in East Forty-ninth Street, New York.

than our architects have yet been able to study it, but larger features, such as bay-windows, porches, and the like, which are matters of course, and which every owner thinks he can have if he can pay for them—even these are dangerous things, and are apt to ruin the fronts in which they are embodied. The front given in the Forty-ninth Street house, on p. 27 seems to answer all the requirements of the case: it is rich and complete looking, it argues care and thought on the part of the designer, and no improper parsimony on the part of the owner; and there is nothing attempted in it which our designers do not thoroughly understand or which our workmen are unable to execute.

Old New York Houses, now the Colonnade Hotel, Lafayette Place, New York.

The subject of corner houses must be touched upon briefly. Where the entrance is in the narrower front, the house is not very unlike a house which is wedged in between two others, the only important difference being that the rooms can be lighted from the side, and some slight improvements are thus rendered easy; but it is rather the custom of late years in New York to enter such corner houses in the middle of the wider front; and this brings up the difficulty alluded to above of separating the two main parts of the house too decidedly one from another; with the added inconvenience of direct entrance from the street into the separating hall. Elegant corner houses, twenty-five feet by sixty and thereabouts, are spoiled by having the hall carried athwart them for nearly their whole width, cutting off one-half of the large rooms of the principal floor from the other half by a strip of passage-way, which it is indeed customary to consider as part of the available space for guests, but which is in reality liable to sudden invasion from out of doors. The high-stoop house, with which New York is afflicted for its sins, shows perhaps more of its awkwardness here than in the houses entered at one end. When an entertainment is going on, especially if it is a large one, when the company rather crowds the house, the guests who arrive must pass through the already assembled company, and gain their dressing-rooms as best they may; and in like manner those guests who may wish to depart early have the gauntlet to run once more. This, which was bad in the old houses, is worse in the new. Custom has made it a matter of course to pass, in wet and bedraggled out-of-door garments, through a full-dressed assemblage, but it is none the less a solecism.

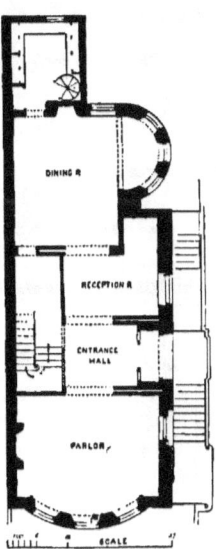

Plan 13.—Corner House on West End Avenue, New York.

Plan 13 * shows what must be a delightful house to live in; and the staircase here is retired enough to make it much better for daily use than it would be if open to the entrance-hall; but here there is still no remedy provided for that awkward arrival and departure of guests, threading their tortuous way through a crowded party. Really, our wealthy New Yorkers ought to remember that their houses are not to live in only. They are to

* House on West End Avenue, Babb, Cook & Willard, architects.

"entertain" in too, and that to an extent hardly reconcilable with right reason. If, therefore, the thronged receptions and dancing-parties are to be made as agreeable as their nature allows, the houses must really be planned with some regard to their requirements.

But, apart from this, what a good plan we have here, and how charming in its simplicity is the exterior, shown in the picture on the opposite page. It is not the object of this paper to dwell upon details, else there would be many things to praise in this design; but mention must be made at least of the treatment of all the faces as parts of the same design— front, side, and rear all of the same material and treated in the same fashion. It is an elementary truth that a corner house will not be a good design if it has a "front" faced with ashlar, a "gable" or end wall faced with Philadelphia brick, and a rear wall of cheaper brick; and yet sumptuous houses are built on that principle to-day.

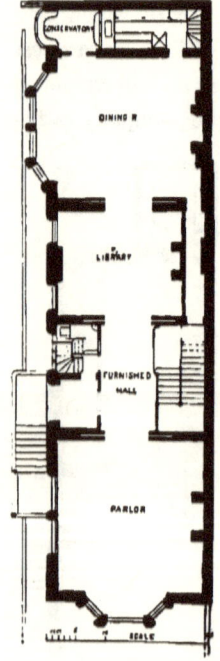

Plan 14.—House in Fifth Avenue, New York.

Plan 14 * shows a simple remedy for some of the troubles we have been considering, namely, a staircase, narrow, but sufficiently easy and spacious for the purpose, carried up direct from the vestibule of the front door to the second story, and equally capable of being carried down to the basement. By means of this, both ladies and gentlemen, on arriving at the house, may go direct to the dressing-rooms provided for them. A very slight extension of the plan would allow of an elevator having the same relation to the first and second stories; but, as to the staircase, it is to be observed that such a ready communication as this between the front door and the upper and lower stories is desirable on

* House in Fifth Avenue, designed by Robert H. Robertson, architect.

other accounts as well. A similar feature is to be seen in large English country houses, where what is called the "bachelors' stair" communicates directly from out of doors to the bedrooms above, enabling

House in West End Avenue, New York.

men who come, wet or muddy, from out-of-door sports, to seek their bedrooms without passing up the great staircase. Such accessories and facilities as this have been too much neglected in our American houses hitherto.

There is no doubt, however, that the real difficulty is in the high-stoop house itself, which is a survival of early and simpler habits, and should have been abandoned long ago for all city dwellings. There is an anomaly, which only long custom blinds us to, in the coming of a porter with a great package or a messenger boy with a note, and his waiting for ten minutes, while an answer is being prepared, within three feet of the door which opens into the drawing-room, which may at that moment be devoted to a large and dressy assembly. It is almost equally objectionable during the hours of family tranquillity; though, as the rooms are not crowded at such times, the door of communication can be shut. There may be a sufficient reason for the retention of the old high-stoop plan in small houses, in which there would not be many entertainments held, and none of a ceremonious kind; but the moment that rich men begin to build houses for their wives and daughters to use in costly entertainment, that moment the plan should have been abandoned once for all. Nothing more incongruous than our New York palaces, of which the first notable one was the marble structure at the corner of Fifth Avenue and Thirty-fourth Street has ever been planned or erected. They are in almost all respects small houses looked at through a magnifying glass; the necessary conditions of a stately house, a sort of palazzo, have hardly been considered in them; the American citizen whose fortune has increased a hundredfold builds a house perhaps tenfold larger than he would otherwise have done, but in other respects very similar to that one in which his father lived in days of comparative poverty.

In closing this examination it will be well to show at least one bold departure from the accepted method of proceeding. Plan 15 shows the first story, and a vertical section of a house* in which many of the disadvantages of our ordinary New York houses are avoided. The treatment of the front and back building in intimate connection with one another below, and wholly separate above, is excellent, and reminds the student of two very dissimilar, but in their way equally successful, types, namely, that of the German and the

* House designed by Thayer & Robinson, architects.

Flemish houses of the sixteenth and seventeenth centuries, a survival itself of an earlier form; and secondly, that of a host of London houses, of which one of the best instances is given in Mr. Kerr's book, "The English Gentleman's House." In the English scheme, the back building contains only the stables on the ground floor, opening into a mews in the rear of the house, and rooms above for the coachman and stable help, while the main building in front has seven

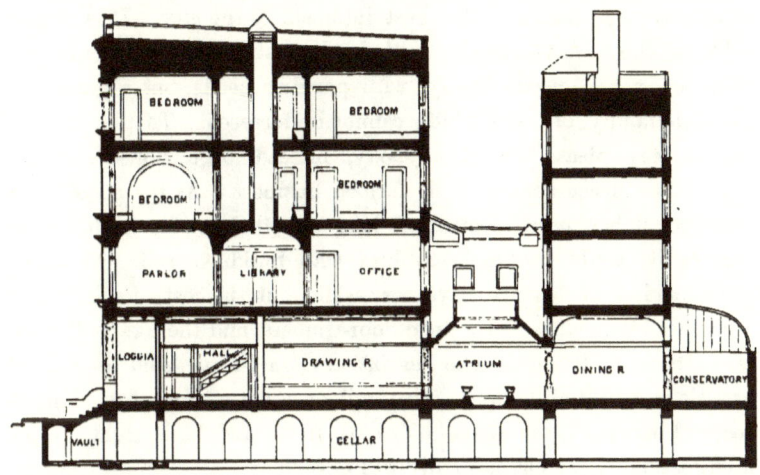

Plan 15.—Section and Plan of a Modern New York House, showing partial separation of front and back buildings.

available stories, namely, the ground floor, which is six steps above the sidewalk; a basement below it, of which only a small part is used for cellarage; and not less than five stories above. This, however, is a detail. The house may be larger or smaller. The theory of giving light to all the rooms by cutting a court for light boldly through the house, and dividing it thus into a front and a rear building, is one that should have been put into practice before this. The other peculiarities in the house, Plan 15, need study, and it is only after several such houses shall have been built that these can be judged aright. Thus, the loggia at the entrance seems to us a mistake, not likely to be useful, and certainly objectionable in several ways. On the other hand, the placing of the kitchen above the dining-room in the back building, would probably work very well.

Unfortunately, it is not New York that will solve such problems. The custom so prevalent in that city of building houses in blocks, and on general principles, for sale to whomsoever will buy, is, of course, preclusive of any originality in treatment, or of the application of any thought and skill to delicacy of plan and arrangement. This fashion is in every way hostile to the best interests of the city. It is impossible for the architect to plan with his best skill when he has to provide for, not a special family, with peculiar needs, but a general, a possible family, of tastes which cannot be foreseen. To plan a house which may please almost anybody, instead of a house specially adapted to please somebody, is forlorn business. As for good building, too, it has been ascertained long ago that solidly built houses cannot be made profitable to him who builds to sell. A certain popular kind of elegance pays very well; but the cost of solid brickwork, well-built flues, extra deep floor-timbers, and the like, will never come back to the man who has invested in them. And as for the artistic side of it all, a speculative builder is not a lover of good architectural ornament, nor does he believe in it; and he is right. Good architectural ornament assuredly will never pay.

It is often pointed out how much a city is injured by the existence within its limits of a large amount of leasehold property; because houses on leased ground will not be so well built as those on freehold ground. But, indeed, houses built by their expectant inhabitants on leased lots would be far better for New York than houses built for sale on land held in fee simple. The one thing needful is that relation between the owner and his property and between the owner and the architect which will result in a house specially fitted to be the home of its owner's family, and of such general design and ornamentation as is best suited to the plan. The architects will meet their employers more than half way; but the initiative must come from the owner—from the man who wants a house.

THE CITY HOUSE IN THE WEST

By JOHN W. ROOT*

THE conditions attending the development of architecture in the West have been, in almost every respect, without precedent. At no time in the history of the world has a community covering such vast and yet homogeneous territory developed with such amazing rapidity, and under conditions of civilization so far advanced. Few times in history have ever presented so impressive a sight as this resistless wave of progress, its farthermost verge crushing down primeval obstacles in nature and desperate resistance from the inhabitants; its deeper and calmer waters teeming with life and full of promise more significant than has ever yet been known. Between the period of conquest and the period of realization there is for art in this great development a distinct hiatus. It is a long time full of deadness, except of physical force, then a sudden bursting of art into exuberant flower. Up to a time twenty years ago every energy of the hardy

---

* John Wellborn Root was born in Georgia, January 10, 1850. His mind proved rarely endowed artistically, with special leanings toward architecture and music. After being graduated at the University of New York he studied in the offices of architects in New York and Chicago. (To Chicago he removed after the fire.) In 1873 he formed a copartnership with Daniel H. Burnham, a fellow-draughtsman, becoming the designer in the new firm of Burnham & Root. Mr. Root was the first representative in Chicago of the new movement in architecture, and was compelled to do much pioneer work which did not fairly express him. In fact his numerous commercial structures scarcely gave congenial opportunity to a mind singularly poetic, and he was just grasping the finer chances when death snatched them from him. Yet his office buildings attain beauty

pioneers who were opening the vast district now called "the West" was expended in the most rudimentary work—that demanded by self-protection and self-support. Even now, in remoter districts, still sounds the Indian's war-whoop, and still exists something of those wild and barbaric conditions so recently conquered farther East.

During the period of this ceaseless struggle architecture, as we understand it, was not thought of; and the most primitive log-hut served for shelter. But as cities began to spring up, the "balloon-framed" wood house was evolved. This early type of dwelling has made the growth of the West possible. Frail as its structure seems to be, it has been the very fortress of civilization, withstanding all assaults of heat and cold, and often baffling the deadly cyclone where massive structures of masonry succumbed. Nothing could be more simple than its skeleton. Unlike the early dwellings of wood erected in the East, no expert carpenter was needed—not mortise nor tenon nor other mysteries of carpentry interfered with the swiftness of its growth. A keg of nails, some two by four inch studs, a few cedar

through that strict adherence to structural truth which was the cardinal point in his creed as an architect. In several—notably the Kansas City Board of Trade and the Woman's Temple in Chicago—the commercial idea is ennobled by a higher aspiration, making these structures among the most beautiful of tall commercial buildings. The first Art Institute, now occupied by the Chicago Club, is one of his most poetic designs, and numerous private dwellings attest the delicacy and diversity of his invention. In the autumn of 1890 he was appointed architect-in-chief of the Columbian Exposition, and in conjunction with Olmsted & Co., landscape architects, he made the general design for the grounds and buildings at Jackson Park. The artistic impulse which achieved the beauty of the Fair was due to Messrs. Burnham & Root, who generously induced the directors to intrust the buildings to the ablest of their professional compeers, and thus established at the outset the national character of the great enterprise. Just before the first meeting of this board of architects Mr. Root fell ill of pneumonia, and died January 15, 1891, aged forty-one. He was a man of varied gifts and great personal magnetism, a fluent and witty speaker, a facile writer in prose and verse, an acute critic, and endowed with lovable and generous qualities. It was said by a famous pianist that "A great musician was lost when John Root took to architecture;" and a great architect, an artist of original genius and rare imaginative power, was lost to America by his early death.

posts for foundations, and a lot of clapboards, with two strong arms to wield the hammer and saw—these only were needed, and these were always to be had. For no sooner did the yell of the Indian grow distant upon the verge of the prairie, or over the slope of the hill, even if but for a few days, than its fierce sound was followed by the drowsy buzz of the saw-mill. Even to-day many Western cities, not only like Chicago, whose earliest growth dates back fifty years, but like Duluth, Minneapolis, Omaha, and others of later growth, are more than half made up of these frame houses. In Chicago the great West Side contains thousands of them. Their life, however, is now nearly finished; for in nearly every Western city of more than one hundred thousand inhabitants the law is passed that within city limits no wood house may be built; so that the next five years will see their total disappearance in favor of more or less substantial structures of masonry.

Thus these hardy pioneers of architecture, in their very disappearance, do architecture some service, for because of them every old Western city must be almost entirely rebuilt, and this under modern and enlightened auspices, as if it had been devastated by a great fire or cyclone. This is clearly an advantage to architecture and to civilization; that is, it may be a great advantage to architecture and to civilization. It certainly presents possibilities to the architects of the West such as have never been given to any other group of men. But with these advantages, it must be confessed, are disadvantages equally palpable; for it is evident that, by virtue of its ephemeral character, the "balloon-framed" house must in nearly all cases fail to become the landmark, venerated for itself, the embodiment of tradition, a monument to the conservatism of a city's history. And similarly it can never become a link in the architectural development of the country.

With the increase of population, wealth, and railroad communication this early dwelling, still retaining its essential structure, grew into more ambitious expression. Its owner, following either his own taste or the equally untrained taste of the most available carpenter or "mill man," adorned it with all sorts of "ornamental" devices in woodwork—open-work scrolls under and above its gables, jig-sawed crestings on its ridges, and wonderful frostings and finials on its gables. The architraves about its windows were no longer content to be of simple boards, but were decorated by rosettes, star-shaped ornaments, and all kinds of forms, suggestive of nothing so much as "nudels" in a German soup. The clapboards or matched ceiling covering it were laid in all directions, sometimes horizontally, as often diagonally in one or two directions, or else in basket fashion, the joints being at right angels with each other. The verandas of these houses offered best opportunity for such display, and here jig-sawed railings and curiously turned or chamfered frosts ran riot.

This obvious and cheap form of decoration, by which a "plain" house was made "tasty" or "modern" to the citizen, persisted for many years. In wood, it was applied with great freedom to cornices and porches of houses built otherwise of stone, when such ambitious structures first began to appear; and forms thus originated in wood were afterward continued in metal, or even in stone itself. Perhaps this fashion gave to Western city houses of twenty years ago a gayer but less substantial appearance than was presented by Eastern houses of the same kind.

In Chicago, previous to the great fire of 1871, the typical city house, whether of wood or stone, or of both combined (for often a stone front was but a mask covering a structure in every other respect of wood), was in general arrangement not unlike the corresponding house in New York. There was the same high "stoop" covering the basement entrance, the same double front and vestibule doors with their transoms, the same narrow hallway with a straight flight of stairs separated from the entrance only by space for the hat-tree, and the front and rear parlors on one side, sometimes with an L in the rear. The street aspect of such houses was different, however, in that it was, as it has been said, gayer and less solid. This effect was produced partly by the freedom with which wood, or wood-like stone or metal decorations were applied, and partly because the stone generally employed was a light limestone, turned with age to a beautiful buff, somewhat like the French Caen stone, which was in sharp contrast with the dark sandstone so commonly employed in the East.

Reference has been made to certain wood-like stone decorations. One who has not seen these translations of wood into stone cannot understand how strange and weirdly interesting they were. Thus, for instance, a large dwelling in Chicago, built twenty years ago at a cost of more than one hundred thousand dollars, is so designed that every person not informed supposes that the highly ornate cornice is of stone and the equally ornate bay-windows are of wood; while the reverse is the case, as is revealed once in five years or so (when the painter is called), when people laboring under the delusion are astonished to find a stone cornice being painted and wood bay-windows cleaned with water.

Bay-windows were, and still remain, a great feature of Western city houses. Their use has been almost universal; sometimes octagonal, sometimes square or segmental, sometimes round placed upon the corner. The customary form twenty years ago, in Chicago at least, was a segmental bay, carried from the ground up to the top of the roof, which generally embraced three stories, this with the high basement being the maximum height of dwelling reached.

Because of the general crudity and haste of things, the architectural methods of this (to the West) early period were sometimes very remarkable. Complete drawings for dwellings to cost, say ten to fifteen thousand dollars, frequently consisted merely of plans and elevations drawn on a scale of one-quarter inch to one foot, supplemented by full-size sections of door and window architraves traced upon sheets of fool's-cap, and copied from the published catalogues of planing-mills. To vary the profile of a moulding from these published catalogues was, in this early day, considered a species of crime, because it entailed upon the manufacturer the cost of new "knives," and the old mouldings were, in any event, good enough for any person except an architectural prig. The width of these architraves and the number of mouldings used to form them were in direct ratio to the cost of the house; so that a very costly dwelling would have a group of mouldings about its doors and windows aggregating twelve, or often fifteen inches in width, these being sometimes made of alternating lines of different and strongly contrasted hard-woods, producing a most bizarre effect. Such an important feature as the main-stairway, with its newels, would be, in the specifications, described somewhat as follows (reference again being had to the published catalogue): "Main newel-post in front hall to be a twelve-inch diameter octagonal newel, heavily moulded, and enriched top and bottom. The hand-rail to be a 'double toad-back' rail, richly moulded, and four by five inches in section; the balusters to be octagon in shape, three inches in diameter, and heavily moulded." Notice the size of these things, and the splendor suggested by the constant recurrence of the word "heavily moulded."

Newspapers in these early days contained advertisements of houses for sale, which, beyond attractions such as are above set forth, would be stated to possess "stationary wash-basins in every room"—this before the days of adequate traps and ventilation. And yet some of the purchasers of these houses and some of their families did not die of malaria.

From the above general remarks St. Louis, Cincinnati, and Louisville must be somewhat excepted. These cities belong as much to the South as to the West. They began an earlier development, and hence were in closer touch with the East at an earlier period than cities farther north. The old city houses peculiar to them were, for this reason, of a much more conservative type than existed in cities like Chicago; and the frame house had not with them acquired the same importance.

The Cincinnati house illustrated on the opposite page, built about twenty years ago, with its simple and dignified stone front, its surrounding stone balustrades, and the general air of family seclusion and repose is a very pleasant object to gaze upon, strongly reminding one of several old houses on Madison Avenue in New York, and of some facing the Public Gardens in Boston, the essential difference being

Old House in Cincinnati, O.

that the Cincinnati house is constructed of light limestone, while those in Boston and New York are of dark sandstone. I think it will be considered that the persistence of this style of house in the older cities of America for so many years has been a very remarkable fact. It has dominated New York, Boston, and Philadelphia with scarcely a variation; and yet, in view of much of the work now being done in these same cities, as well as in cities of the West, we may be grateful that the style was more inoffensive. Beside some of its younger brothers it becomes very much the fine gentleman.

Both Cincinnati and St. Louis are cities where, although summer weather is very hot, very cold weather is frequently experienced in winter. It seems strange, therefore, that a house plan [No. 1] should be so largely used as that which is published herewith; and yet, with all the inconvenience attached to the absence of a hallway leading to the rear bedrooms, this plan is very common in both cities.

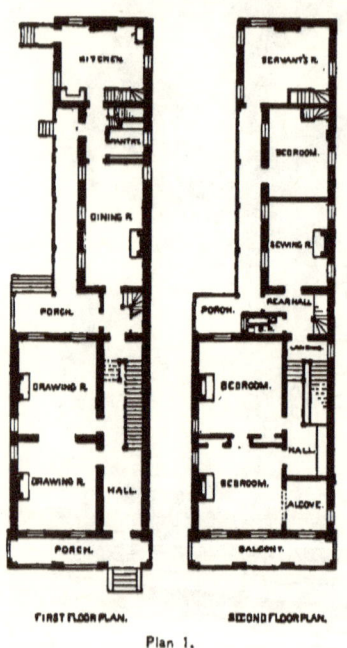

Plan 1.

These cities, with Louisville, have architectural traditions and histories extending back, as we have said, much farther than other Western cities, but they seldom present objects of interest for the purpose of this paper, as they are, in the main, in direct sympathy with, or direct copies of, Eastern work, and present few aspects of local or typical interest. To these there are a few exceptions. In Cincinnati there is an old one-story dwelling, built in strongly defined Colonial feeling, which is so elegant in its proportions and details, so refined in its entire expression, that it is worth a pilgrimage to see. The Grecian columns of the portico, with their strongly accented entases, and the general treatment of cornice and window architraves, is strongly suggestive of many of the old houses about New Bedford and Newburyport. The house is unfortunately so embowered in trees that a photograph of a representative kind was impossible; although, in truth, to take a photograph of such a house would seem almost as impertinent as to insult a fine old maid by capturing her picture with a "Kodak" without her knowledge.

St. Louis, also, has in several of the older streets (Lucas Place, for instance) two or three old dwellings of interest. Two I recall, built of buff limestone, which have with age turned into a lovely scheme of color, varying from delicate old ivory to a rich "meerschaum brown;" and the entire surface of the stone is encrusted with delicate lichen and other vegetable growth, as beautifully and minutely traced as are the needles of ice first formed on still water.

Chicago possessed a few interesting souvenirs of its early history; but these, alas! went with the great fire of 1871; and scarcely a remnant remains; and of these few not one has been spared by the irreverent hand of progress.

From the early and meagre architectural development of this and other Western cities the present state is vastly removed. Indeed, modern Western dwellings seem to have scarcely a visible trace of relationship to these earlier types. First, let it be noted that there is in Western cities a notable absence, compared with cities in the East, of houses built in blocks. The reason for this is obvious. Eastern cities being older, were begun and their traditions established at a time when their citizens were more interdependent, and facilities for transportation were less complete than now. For this reason they are not only more compactly built, but ground has become dearer than in the West. The reverse is true of Western cities, and the result is that residences much more frequently occupy considerable space, being entirely detached from other houses and surrounded by their own trees and lawns. It will frequently happen that a citizen imbued with characteristic and full confidence in the future growth of his city will purchase a large tract slightly removed from the business centre, upon which he will build his home, knowing that but a short time will elapse before it will be embraced by the city itself. When this occurs, he subdivides and sells what he does not need, reserving an acre or two for his own purposes. The frequency of this kind of thing gives Western dwellings a general suburban aspect, removing them from the class of city houses to which we may have become accustomed. This suburban effect is also enhanced by the extraordinary increase in the variety of building materials, which, coupled with the characteristic Western love of novelty, often leads to the erection of houses as different in material, color, and treatment as is possible to conceive, different dwellings in the same street being as independent of each other—often as apparently hostile as if separated by wide stretches of open country.

Nevertheless, many streets thus built up present a superb air of space, comfort, and even luxury. In driving through these streets the eye is at no time wearied with the monotony which is so tiresome in Fifth Avenue or other similar streets in Eastern cities, but is everywhere delighted with constant change, constant appeal to new sentiment, and that delightful sense of the picturesque which, to the stranger, is so inspiring. Notable among such streets are Euclid Avenue in Cleveland, where the splendid residences which line it are often set back as much as two or three hundred feet from the street; Michigan Boulevard and the Lake Shore drive in Chicago, superbly paved streets with great variety of interesting outlook; Prospect and Grand Avenues in Milwaukee, the first overlooking the lake from a bluff one hundred feet high, the second a magnificently wooded avenue two hundred feet wide; and several avenues in St. Paul, Minneapolis, and other cities. Occasionally these streets are laid out park-wise, still further accenting this suburban aspect. Such are to be found in St. Louis, in Van Deventer Place; in Cincinnati, in Walnut Hills and Clifton, where, with winding roadways and magnificent trees, all the beauty of the country is brought into immediate contact with city life. This rusticity is by no means universal, but it is so common as to give a distinct quality to Western cities, and by contrast to impress one, in older towns, like Cincinnati and St. Louis, with a certain Eastern flavor, when passing through their old, solidly and uniformly built-up portions.

Even where dwellings occur solidly built into blocks there is an equally distinctive effect produced by means in some ways identical with those used in detached houses. The great variety of building material accessible, freely and indiscriminately employed in a block of residences, produces at times an effect most bizarre and startling. Such blocks attain their most flamboyant expression—if "all which flams is flamboyant"—in the large number of dwellings built by real-estate speculators for sale. The inducement in Western cities to erect such houses, because of the wonderful increase in real-estate values, is very great; while the temptation to catch the eye of the possible purchaser by unknown and unheard-of novelty is to the builder irresistible. The result is that in a block constructed with this end in view, one house may be of red sandstone, the next of gray, the next of green, and so on. Meanwhile, each house has its own bays of copper; its own cornice, turrets, and other "fixings" of galvanized iron; its own carved panels of terra-cotta; which, with bands of pressed brick, porches of wood, aprons, roofs, and "rooflets" of slate and tiles, make up an *olla podrida* most trying to even the sturdiest of stomachs.

Against such barbarism a wholesome reaction has set in, and nowhere may simpler and more honestly built dwellings be found than many now erected and erecting in the West. It may be prophesied with certainty that, as a result of the architectural movement now in progress, Western cities like Chicago, St. Louis, Kansas City, Minneapolis, Milwaukee, and many others will, within a short time, present streets unrivalled in the world for the variety, picturesqueness, and beauty of their domestic architecture.

In this chapter no reference is made to very costly dwellings. These are not apt to be illustrative of popular taste so much as to be the representative of the personal taste and whim of the owner or architect, striving to impress itself by splendor or idiosyncrasy upon those passers-by who might otherwise be indifferent or untouched. The illustrations chosen are from houses of moderate expense, costing from ten to forty thousand dollars.

Perhaps, since the interior plan of the house is its vital part, from which everything else grows, it may be well to give a few representative plans which have been developed in Western houses. In the growth of the house-plan from the earlier types the first great change began with the hall. This, originally a narrow passage, of no service for living and with few possibilities for decorative treatment, has been expanded, and made of practical value in several ways, becoming not only a large and picturesque room of itself, but serving admirably as a general reception-room or *rendezvous* for family and guests. Sometimes this reception-room is placed upon the street level, in other cases it is raised above the street by a number of steps, which may be placed either within the front entrance or without it, as in the case of old-fashioned "stoops." In small houses the first arrangement presents obvious advantages (see Plans 2 and 3). The reception-hall is here convenient to the street, offering that immediate shelter to the guest which in rough weather is so desirable, and the opportunity to adjust himself before meeting the host or other guests who may have already arrived. The hall's remoteness from the main or living portion of the house saves those within from the noise and draughts incident to the opening of the hall-door. This arrangement also leaves the living story in much more available shape, es-

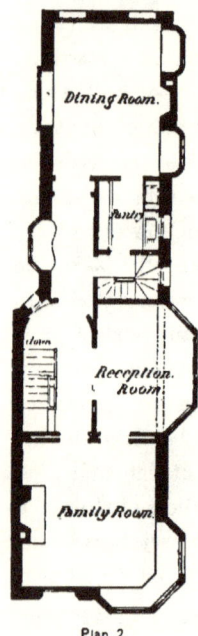

Plan 2.

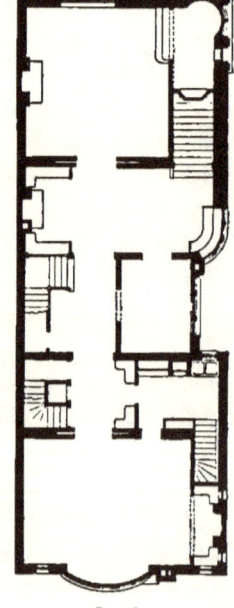

Plan 3.

pecially in the front room, which may be extended the full width of the house.

Of these plans, that marked No. 2 is simpler than No. 3, but less picturesque. In Plan 2 the reception-hall has a fireplace of brick, and oak floor and oak panelled ceiling; a toilet-room opens from it, and coat closet. The room is bright and cosey, presenting a cheerful and reassuring aspect to the stranger and a homelike welcome to the owner.

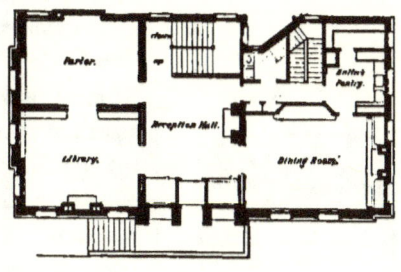

Plan 4.

Plan 3 is very ingenious and picturesque. The entrance proper is from a loggia, which may be inclosed in winter, and in this plan less stress is placed upon the reception-room in the *rez-de-chaussée* than in Plan 2. The hall is on the principal floor, and gives a very picturesque view of the stairs and the other rooms about it. Its disadvantage is in the fact that it offers no seclusion to guests arriving at a reception and before removing their wraps—a criticism almost equally true of Plans 4 and 5.

The hall in Plan 4 is simple and obvious, presenting many advantages of convenience and beauty. The inconvenient location of the stairs, in case of receptions, has been, in another house of similar plan, removed by enlarging the hall somewhat and placing the stairs to the left of the entrance, doing away with the two alcoves. Wide windows upon the stair-landing between the first and second stairs, together with groups of windows in the opposite or north wall, give adequate light to the hall. In this house the mantel is made more monumental in design, and is placed nearly opposite the entrance.

The hall in Plan 5 is very effective. The first stair-landing is placed at the intersection of the three axes of the adjacent rooms, so as to be equally visible from each of them, and to present a very picturesque glimpse of each of them, and by this means some very charming effects are obtained. It will be seen that two of the rooms present a view in perspective, so that the front and sides of all large pieces of furniture are equally seen, producing an effect somewhat unusual in the arrangement of dwellings.

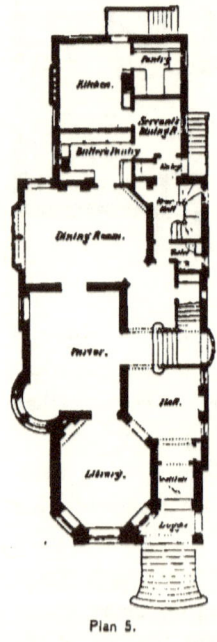

Plan 5.

In the growth of their plans Western city houses have tended also toward greater enlargement and importance of the living and dining-rooms, at the expense of the parlor and reception-rooms. Of course, reference is made to houses of moderate cost. The old fashion, in which the largest and brightest rooms were reserved for occasional guests, while the family lived in small and ill-lighted apartments, seems happily over, and now the brightest rooms, containing the most picturesque street aspects, will generally be found to be rooms of commonest use. The few plans here illustrated suggest this idea. For instance, the front rooms in Plans 2 and 3 are living-rooms, and the parlors or reception-rooms are the small, less desirable rooms in the centre of the house. The library, or living-room, in Plan 5 is the octagonal room giving a view upon the street; and Plan 4 would be improved, from the average Western stand-point, were the library made larger and the drawing-room smaller. The words "library" and "living-room" are made interchangeable, because in general the library is the living-room, which, being thus made much larger than other rooms, admits of treatment much freer and broader than they. Its wealth of books and pictures, *bric-à-brac*, portfolios; its roomy tables and easy-chairs, its generous, wide-throated fireplace, the general air of profusion and informality, revealing something of the true character of the occupant to be brought into intimate

House in Prairie Avenue, Chicago, Ill.

contact with, which is so delightful to the guest—all make this the attractive room of the house. Here is the focus of family gatherings, the inspiration of wit and good-fellowship, and the opportunity fully to express the true character of family tastes and accomplishments.

The dining-room has also greatly gained in dignity and importance, its size, shape, aspect, the reception of the morning sunshine, its coloring and entire sentiment are all carefully considered.

One feature in the plans of Western city dwellings must be very clearly defined. This is their openness. Not only are windows upon the average larger than in the East, but they are more frequent, as are also bay-windows, oriels, etc.; while in the general plan rooms are more closely related, openings between rooms wider, and single swinging-doors less frequent. Several dwellings in Chicago—and there are many in other Western cities—have no doors whatever in the first story, except those at the entrance and between the dining-room and butler's pantry, curtains being exclusively used. This is certainly carrying out the idea of openness to the extreme, as it is the destruction of all privacy, and of all those suggestive glimpses upon which so much of the artistic effect of a house depends.

A small room has intruded itself upon many Western city houses, which should be lamented equally by the occupant and the architect. This is a kind of office or den, where the master of the house keeps a desk and a few facilities for the transaction of business after hours are over in which business should be transacted; for in the enormous pressure of events about him the Western man, perhaps even more than his brother in the East, is compelled in the evenings to carry something of his business across the threshold of his house.

As in the East, that chief minister to the ethical side of the family life, the fireplace, has steadily grown in beauty and dignity, until now it has regained something of the supremacy from which it was threatened with dethronement when first the source of heat and comfort was inaugurated in the shape of a black hole in the floor. It is now apt to be most generous in size, wide enough for a good back log, and richly adorned with marbles or tiles, equipped with carefully designed firedogs, fenders, and screens. These fireplaces have become things of service as well as things of beauty. Woe betide the hapless architect who builds them in such fashion that the smoke goes the wrong way. No felicitous retort may save him; no soft answer can turn away wrath. It is said of Richardson that a very valuable client gave him commission to build for him a house more or less ideal, the ideally-ideal feature of which was to be a grand, guaranteed-not-to-smoke dining-room fireplace. All architects will at once guess that this fireplace performed prodigies in the way of smoking out the inhabitants. At the house-warming dinner, at which Richardson was present, every eye had wept scalding tears because of it. After the dinner the host turned to Richardson and said, with great suavity, "Your fireplace smokes you see;" and Richardson said, "Yes, I see it does; but don't you like it?"

Take the subject of Western city house plans altogether, it will be found that from 1874 to within a few years back there was a tendency toward all sorts of ingenious arrangements producing odd and startling effects; but since then a reaction has set in toward simpler and more practical plans, in which space, light, and utility supplant mere eccentricity.

Viewed from without, many interesting developments will be noticed.

Of course the West took "the Queen Anne" fever with alarming intensity. It was just at the tender age when the constitution is most sensitive to such infantile diseases, and during its prevalence eruptions of all sorts came out in the most extraordinary way. But the youth of the patient was in its favor and the fever fortunately passed away, and now manifests itself in only a few cases, such as were mentioned earlier in this article. H. H. Richardson was one of the most efficient physicians in working the cure, for under his influence such architects as had been following Norman Shaw (blindly and ignorantly, as they had followed him) turned from him and began to follow the American. The results have been in many cases very happy, although in others they have resulted more or less disastrously. Richardson's influence has always tended to make architecture more simple and direct, and it has led architects more generally to avoid the hideous mass of shams which in America preceded him. Among results

House on Dearborn Avenue, Chicago, Ill.

upon the whole fortunate is the use of quarry-faced stone in Western dwellings. The extent to which this has been done in nearly every Western city is extraordinary, and so accustomed to stone in this shape have people become that they often seem unable to realize that cut stone has at times greater artistic value. Many dwellings constructed in this rough material have an exceeding heavy and forbidding look, arising in large part because in them stone has been employed in blocks too large for the scale of the building, or because granite has been used whose cleavage has left too strongly projecting and rugged surfaces. This was a mistake which Richardson, in the few Western houses he has designed, has avoided; his fine sense of scale saving him from such an error. Still it must be confessed that, because of the great vigor and masculinity of his genius, he was generally more successful in monumental buildings than in smaller dwellings. His blind followers have often failed where he succeeded, because they were denied his finer sense.

Successful dwellings constructed of this material are, as might be inferred, generally very simple in detail; few mouldings are used either at window-jambs or elsewhere; even arches are sparingly employed, and carving is applied very temperately. In the more frequent examples the general effect is simple, dignified, and satisfactory. The main entrance is in nearly every case the centre of the entire composition, and the place upon which is bestowed greatest enrichment. One of the most satisfactory of these dwellings is illustrated on p. 53. This is built of a reddish-brown sandstone, slightly mottled with gray, and having a cleavage not too rounded for satisfactory wall surfaces. The general composition of the building is very good, and the doorway is recessed within a well-sheltered loggia. The general mass and color of the building is altogether pleasing.

Among the abuses arising from the use of quarry-faced stone it may be well to mention what seems to be a peculiarly Western institution, the quarry-faced column. This is built of blocks of rough stone piled upon each other, and is the most distressing architectural plague since the plagues of the other sort in Egypt. The stone surfaces never come in line with each other, the column, therefore, never seems straight, and the joints, being all recessed, give it the effect of a soft bag banded with strings. As an ideal expression, therefore, of absolute instability it is among all architectural forms unrivalled.

Cut stone has been employed comparatively seldom in the West since the earlier days when ashlar was largely used which had been put upon a rubbing-bed and brought to a perfectly smooth surface.

The use of stone in more vigorous expression has almost entirely taken its place. The rougher dressing of stone occurs in comparatively few cases. This is perhaps partly a matter of expense and partly the result of an ephemeral taste which may change.

Brick and terra-cotta are more largely employed than stone work in

House on Dearborn Avenue, Chicago, Ill.

nearly every Western city, and both are manufactured in variety practically without limit. Bricks of every conceivable color may be found, and terra-cotta to harmonize with them. I have seen bricks manufactured in the West having the exact effect of green mosses, or the various tones given by small flowers and lichens adhering to stone, or else having surfaces black and burnished with metallic lustres.

Such material as this opens out possibilities for color treatment such as had not been dreamed of, which will doubtless be productive of many startling and distressing effects before architects shall have obtained the entire mastery of this nicest of all arts, the art of color. Such materials have contributed largely to the dwelling-house development of the West.

The Dearborn Avenue house, illustrated on p. 55, is built of brick and terra-cotta in very satisfactory dull red. All the details of this house are modelled with singular crispness and vigor, and the fine rococo sentiment is carefully preserved. This is one of the best houses, in many ways, designed for a position within a continuous block, in Chicago.

The State Street dwelling, on p. 57, is built of Roman bricks of deep brown, with lines of red running through them, and the terra-cotta is made in the same general coloring. The entire effect of the wall is very satisfactory in possessing a singular bloom of color entirely different and much richer than if each brick in the wall had been in one tone. This house has a very strong colonial feeling, without in any way servilely following the Colonial type.

Bricks are used in the Prairie Avenue house, p. 49, which are made of fire-clay burnt to vitrification. Their colors are warm golden browns, with very considerable variety, the surface being slightly rough. A more pleasing wall it will be difficult to conceive, and the bricks so burned have the rare advantage of being impervious to water and frost, and of maintaining their color and quality intact for an indefinite period of time. This dwelling illustrates the growth of an English feeling similar to that shown in some of the new London houses in Cadogan Square, Harrington Gardens, and elsewhere.

The Bellevue Place house [p. 59] is built, in the first story, of reddish-brown rough-faced brick.

It will be observed that in the West, as in the East, the roof seems to have come to stay. Its frank expression, and its free use as a most important element in design is everywhere seen. This is most promis-

House in North State Street, Chicago, Ill.

ing for city architecture, where nothing so much adds to the interest of street vistas as outlines of high-pitched and well-modelled roofs.

Especial attention is called to the St. Louis dwelling on p. 60. This is of such unusual picturesqueness, and is so simple and direct in design as to be thoroughly charming. Nothing in the exterior design is adventitious; the design grows naturally out of the plan. Notice the quaint dignity of the whole, and think how delightful would be the aspect of our cities if such dwellings as this, with their varied outlines of roof and tower and dormer, the strong individuality and harmonious coloring were more frequent. This dwelling also

House in Bellevue Place, Chicago, Ill.

House in St. Louis, Mo.

illustrates how largely suburban in aspect a true city house may be.

The few wooden dwellings which are illustrated show that not yet have they been banished from Western cities; ultimately they will be confined to the suburbs or the country, but at present they often form agreeable variations to the general street aspect. In certain examples they show that the influence of the neo-Colonial has passed to even the distant West, and if it has not always reached its point of greatest refinement, it still shows a vigor of thought and handling. The Milwaukee dwelling [p. 61] presents some novel and pleasing features, especially in the use of the stucco frieze and in the management of the gables.

THE CITY HOUSE IN THE WEST

San Francisco has had a very unusual architectural experience; it has been more isolated from the rest of the country than almost any other of our cities; its development, therefore, has been more peculiarly its own, and has been less modified by contemporaneous work in Eastern cities. It is only of very late years that work being done in the East has strongly modified the feeling of San Francisco architects. The fear of earthquakes has caused nearly every dwelling-house to be constructed of wood. In spite of this fact, little seems to have been done, as might have been expected, toward developing an architecture of wood. All sorts of architectural styles, originating in stone, have been adopted bodily in wood, with scarcely a change in the original stone expression except such as is absolutely necessary for the jointing

House in Milwaukee, Wis.

of a different material. California and other parts of the Pacific coast, are blessed, in so far as their wood houses are concerned, in their beautiful red-wood. This is a lovely color for interior, as well as exterior work. Its effect, when used outside in shingles and otherwise, and treated with spar varnish, is singularly fine, presenting to the eye a fine leathery texture. This wood is not difficult to work, and when used with intelligence and discretion should be made to contribute, to a great degree, in the development of new forms of design in wood.

The houses mentioned above, like all typical Western dwellings, are better finished within than their exterior would seem to indicate. The reverse of this is seldom true, and this is a good deal to say for the certain honesty in Western cities, where the occupant of the house is less interested in making a specious display to his neighbors than in acquiring a solid and enduring comfort for himself. Native hardwoods are freely used, especially white and red oak, both quartered and plain. These woods have been especially popular; their beautiful grain and open texture lend themselves to so many effects of color that they have taken the place of other wood, the color required being imparted to them by filling and staining; indeed, their use has become so general that the supply threatens to be exhausted, and their market value has increased during the last few years nearly double. From California come several beautiful—if rather showy—woods, in yellows and reds. The manilla-wood from the coast has much of the beauty of mahogany, with its deep red tones and waving grain. Curiously enough, when we have practically abandoned in the West the use of American black walnut, which at one time was employed far more than any other native hard-wood, and are now beginning to use so freely the English oak, the very "swell thing" in England seems to be to abandon the use of their beautiful oak and substitute instead our American black walnut.

Much more may be said of the interior aspect of these Western dwellings, which is as varied as their exterior designs, or as the temperament and social position and disposition of the occupant.

Again let me say, that between the character of the occupant and the general expression of the dwelling there is much greater similarity than in any other part of the country. The one is much less governed by artificial conditions than his brother in the East, and very much more freely expresses himself.

A few years back, and contemporaneous with the reign of, first, the "Victoria Gothic" and afterward the "Queen Anne," was the reign of marvellous wall-paper, portières, *bric-à-brac*, and Eastlake furniture. To all of these the West gave swift obedience. Houses may still be found in abundance where each of these sovereigns holds divided sway; but in the main common-sense has won the day, or at least other and less artificial fads now rule. First the embroidered, carved, painted, cast and wrought iron crane, who so long stood on one leg amid surrounding cat-tails, has died; the death was prolonged and painful, but seems finally to have occurred. After this the famous, honestly constructed, glued-on, mortice-and-tenon furniture fell to pieces and went to the cellar; then, as intelligence increased, the people began to purchase pictures of interest and beauty, and ceased to paste pictures of no interest and beauty on their walls and ceilings. After this came a yearning for more sunlight and fresh air, and heavy stuffs were largely removed from doorways and windows, and lighter materials substituted. Last of all, the indiscriminate vase and plaque, the ubiquitous display of cups and saucers, have given way to temperateness in this as in other things. Even "stained" glass, which in the West has for many years run a most shameless career, has grown less wild and uncivilized, exchanging its barbaric hues for gentler whites and opals.

Take it altogether, the outlook for Western city houses seems most promising. Western people themselves are becoming, and will still more become, almost ideal clients. It is true that, as in the East, Western city dwellings have not escaped the deadly touch of the "know-it-all" client, nor of the man who is "building the house to suit himself," nor of him who "is going to live inside the house, not outside," and who is therefore loftily indifferent to the street aspect of his house; but each, even the last person, is becoming infrequent. In the past, and to some degree at present, Western cities have been and are influenced by men whose lives have been absorbed by things too material to leave them much leisure for art; but even in the case of such men there is a marked indisposition to dictate in directions where their knowledge is incomplete. They have a large openness and unbiased attitude of mind, and a genuine and earnest desire to "get the best." In the West is less often found than in the East the "æsthetic crank," and it is also true that life in the West is less conventional, freer, less restrained by artificial restrictions than in older communities, and the true nature of people and things is perhaps more frankly expressed.

All of these conditions are helps to the architect, for while they free him from such artificialities as might tend to hamper him, or to make his work more formal, they give wholesome impetus to honest and earnest endeavor.

Circumstances are also such that the architect may act with great catholicity. Architectural tradition in the West there is none. Even from such practices as may exist in the East the West will often hesitate to borrow; and among the various Western cities marked tendencies toward divergence not only from the East, but among themselves, may be noted. Thus contemporaneous work in St. Paul and Minneapolis will differ in a marked degree from similar work in Omaha or Denver; and the dwelling-houses now erected in Chicago have marked peculiarities not to be found in other cities. These variations are due to great differences of climate and customs, as well as to differences of temperament among both clients and architects, for the enormous size of "the West" must be borne in mind when considering this great architectural development.

Among these various rival cities dominant fads in architecture are likely to become less common, and problems will be more generally determined by the nature of the case.

House in Denver, Col.

The rivalry among these cities is a most important factor in the growth of domestic as well as commercial architecture. In cases like St. Paul and Minneapolis, every move of either city is watched by the other with keenest interest, and every structure of importance erected in one city becomes only the standard to be passed by the other; so that not only is it their ambition to excel in matters of population and wealth, but also in the splendor and prominence of their architectural movement. It is similar with individuals. Men who in many cases began their careers at the same time, who perhaps came from the same Eastern State, who have together succeeded in careers which seem but integral parts of the great developments about them, have with each other a very earnest but generous emulation, and exercise a careful scrutiny each of the action of the other, not only of his attitude and actions toward the social world but toward the world of art; and the result will inevitably be the growth of better and more wholesome art feeling.

In the beginning instance this desire to surpass begot much of the meretriciousness and display of architectural gewgaws.

This, however, exists no longer. No men travel so much as Westerners. The distance from St. Paul to Boston is less than one-fourth the distance from Boston to St. Paul; San Francisco men drop into Chicago as lightly as a Baltimore man would into New York, and every one of these men knows something about architecture. Indeed, with the intimacy enforced upon him with all forms of building operations, he could not remain ignorant if he chose. Wherever he goes, therefore, his eyes are wide open, and he will in the frankest way express opinions on So-and-So's dwelling in cities far East, often in Berlin or Vienna, at the same time compare them with dwellings more familiar to him and nearer home. Such conditions are certainly significant, and architecture growing up among them cannot fail to be vital.

That this Western architecture is vital cannot be denied. With all its crudity begotten of ignorance, but more often begotten of haste, domestic architecture in the West is certainly vigorous; there can be no question of its insistence upon the right to live. And with this vitality there will not be wanting material with which to work.

House in Minneapolis, Minn.

Not a day passes in the office of any architect of active practice but specimens are brought in of new granite quarried in Wisconsin, new sandstones from Michigan, ricolites from Mexico, verd-antique jaspers and rich marbles from Colorado to California. There is an equally steady current of new processes for art metal-work in bronze and iron, of mosaics in glass and marble, of rich wall-coverings in leather, stuffs, and even stamped wood-pulp, and in new forms of beautiful encaustic materials.

The forces employed in producing every sort of material intended for use in constructing and adorning buildings, especially dwelling-houses, seems infinite. These various things the greater adventure and love of novelty in the West will more freely use than will the East, with consequences both for better and worse. But disastrous experiments remain isolated, since nothing is truer than the general sterility of bad art ventures; the successful efforts will remain and multiply.

With a wholesome quality of mind and life in the layman, and with imagination and discrimination in the architect, what may not our domestic architects become? In twenty years this will be the richest and most luxurious country ever known upon the globe. Shall all of these treasures of nature and of art, all of these fostering environments, result in architecture splendid in material conditions alone, like that of later Rome, or shall it be chiefly distinguished, with all its splendor, by the earnestness, vigor, and thoughtfulness which inspire the whole?

THE SUBURBAN HOUSE

By BRUCE PRICE

DURING the last century, and the first half of the present one, country life in America had assumed a popular and well-defined existence, and through all the old Atlantic States numerous seats and homes had been built that were distinctive and beautiful in character. Many of these, upon the larger estates and in the suburbs of the great cities, were of such size and commanding proportions as to be really mansions. But throughout the country generally, and particularly in and about the important towns and villages, were numerous quiet and well-designed homes resting in their own grounds.

The life in these homes during this period was quite as characteristic as the homes themselves. In the country towns of Virginia, Maryland, Pennsylvania, and the New England States, lived a charming people, who in their ample way dispensed a broad hospitality and made a society, intelligent, refined, and almost chivalric in its intercourse. But the progress and development of the country set many influences at work upon the disintegration of this life. The spread of the great cities razed many of the fine suburban houses; the division of property broke up the country estates and reduced the town's. The war told upon both, and with the wider, broader, more nervous life that followed upon the restoration of peace, the old life soon became almost a myth. Commerce, business, and the race for wealth at once engaged the whole nation; the cities filled and grew, and the country fell away year by year.

House at Mamaroneck, N. Y.
(McKim, Mead & White, Architects.)

The fashion, almost universal at this time with city people, was to spend a few days, or weeks at most, during the heated term, at the great hotels of "the springs," "the summer resort," or the sea-shore. There were many, of course, who, loving the country, sought its quiet, and roughed it on a farm, and a few others who built, and passed their summers in, villas in the suburban country.

But from the whirl and heat of the city, the summer hotel, with its artificial life and huddling quarters, was a poor resource, and early in the seventies the country cottage—a cheap frame nondescript, without cellar or plumbing—began to appear. These cottages were for the most part very simple affairs, built with steep roofs and shallow verandas, and called Gothic. They were the forerunners of a movement that took, at the time, the form almost of a craze. Cramped in the confined quarters of their city houses, with children growing up about them, numbers looked to the country and longed for some place where they could have free air and abundant room. The fever of this desire spread like an epidemic and developed the epoch of the suburban villa cities, with amazing results. About the outlying towns near the great northern cities large tracts of country were laid out in villa sites and coursed with avenues and boulevards, paved and curbed, and bordered with sickly infantile elms and maples. Block upon block of "villas" sprang up, hideous structures of wood, covered with jig-sawed work, with high stoops, and capped with the lately imported so-called French roof; all standing in their own grounds and all planned upon the same *motif*—a city house planted in the country. The traveller nearing New York or Philadelphia went through acres of these villas in all stages of progress, from the raw boards to the gorgeous primary reds, yellows, and greens in which their cheap, vulgar details were glaringly set off.

These villa cities were short-lived; the Centennial Exposition at Philadelphia soon following, brought our people together and showed them many truths. It taught them that back of all the uses of life there could be art in everything. One beautiful truth fell upon many,

Colcott's group of English cottages, the head-quarters of the English Commission to the Exposition, built in half-timbered and shingled work, revealed how lovely a thing a cottage could be when built with artistic intelligence. The influence of these buildings upon both the public and professional mind was, at the time, very great. They showed us not only the ugliness and unfitness of the French-roof villa, but taught us to appreciate, from the example of their own fitness, the merit and beauty of our national work about us on all sides. Colcott, in England, for his inspiration had gone back to the best period of his own national homes. His contemporaries were doing the same. The good of the old was being revived there; and soon the good in the old with us was sought out and studied.

Men whose paths led them through our older towns could not but contrast their quiet beauty with the vulgar incongruity of these mushroom "villa cities." Their broad, turf-bordered roads, with avenues of great trees spanning the way from side to side; and the old white houses, simple in form, refined in detail, broad and generous in plan and treatment; with the yard in front, the garden at rear, the one filled with rose-trees, oleanders, rose-of-Sharon bushes, and box-bordered walks, the other with fruit-trees and hedges, and garden-beds and borders of hollyhocks or sunflowers. Many, going into the nearer accessible towns, found these old homes and made them theirs; while others, feeling the beauty of such places, built upon their lines.

And so the tide turned. The migration back to the country annually became greater and greater, until now, whether these homes are to be permanent or for the summer only, the problem, how properly to build them, is a fixed one for the architect, and fills his thoughts and crowds his boards. Climate and habits of life have clearly marked for him the bounds of the problem. The modest cottage of a few years ago, built to rough it in through the hot days of summer, gives place to the more hospitable home of to-day. This home must be snug and comfortable, with broad hearth-stones and warm walls to shield its tenants through the biting days of autumn and winter. The heat of summer demands shady porches and wide verandas; the cold of winter snug corners and sunny rooms—two opposite conditions to be reconciled under the same roof. The rooms must be wide, with through drafts inviting the cooling winds of summer, yet low studded and shielded against the blasts of winter. The house must be ample for summer guests and summer hospitality, compact for the family gathering around the winter fireside, and home-like at all times.

And these homes—what are they now and what shall they be? Passing them in review we have a retrospect of about seventeen years. The movement taking form, as we have seen, about the Centennial year, matured as we know it to-day. In viewing the work of this period it is not to the point to consider the larger establishments of Newport, Mount Desert, Lenox, or the great places that have been raised up all through different parts of the country; it is either the permanent home or the summer residence of the man of moderately independent means that interests us—houses costing from five to twenty thousand dollars.

In all this work the scheme of the plan, whether the cost be of the less or greater amount, is now almost identical.

The ordinary older cottages, those of a quarter of a century ago, were generally planned with a single entrance facing the approach; this opened from a porch into a passage rather than a hall, with the stairways starting a few paces within and running straight up against the side-wall to the floor above; the parlor and library to right and left, with the dining-room beyond the one and the kitchen beyond the other. Between the last two came the butlery and servants' stairs, and the back-door, which usually in the family life of the occupants became the thoroughfare to and from the house. This, pure and simple, was the general plan from which the house of to-day started. Step by step it developed. First the passage was attacked, and being broadened became a hall; the staircase fell away from near the threshold to a less obtrusive place, with landings and returns, and windows opening upon them. As the hall grew, the parlor, as its uses and purposes were more absorbed by the hall, became of less importance. The fireplace became a prominent feature, and placed in the hall and more elaborately treated, became an ingle-nook, with the mantel over it, forming an imposing chimney-piece. Improving thus its separate features upon the old, the newer plan advanced further in the disposition of these features. The new hall having become broad and ample, and the rendezvous and seat of the home life, took its position in the most desirable place in the advanced plan. The house grew up about it, following with the other features and details in their proper sequence, until now, from the sum of all that has been done, the resulting general plan, with its controlling conditions of site, can be adduced. Resolving these conditions of site again into general conditions, the result of both is this: to plan and place the house upon its site so that the approach and entrance-door shall be upon one side and the lawn and living-rooms upon the opposite. Stating it directly, the best work enables us to approach by a drive upon one side, alight at an entrance-porch, enter by an entrance-hall, advance thence into the hall, and through it out upon the veranda, and so on upon the lawn. This is the simple result, and the reason is as simple. The entrance is for access; the hall, veranda, lawn, and the prospect beyond, belong to the private life of the house. Tradesmen or visitors, however welcome, cannot be dropped into the midst of the family group. Even the welcome guest wishes to cross the threshold and meet the outstretched hand and cordial greeting within. Even Liberty Hall must have its defence.

If the road to the house crosses the lawn and comes at once upon the hall, veranda, and seat of the home life, the home life is open to intrusion at any time. And so it is important to keep these features separate.

As all sites are not alike, so all plans cannot be alike; but knowing the site and studying well the access to and the prospect from it, the intelligent architect can readily arrange his plan to suit. If the approach is from the north, and the site falls off gradually to the south, with the view toward that quarter, then the solution of the problem is simple and direct, and at its best. The house is placed well to the northern boundary, leaving it sufficiently away from the thoroughfare to insure privacy and space for the turn of the drive. The greater portion of the site is thus given to the lawn upon the south side. The house is placed with its long axis east and west, its approach and entrance upon the north side, its living-rooms, hall, veranda, and lawn upon the south, and it stands thus in itself a barrier between the turmoil of the world and the peace and privacy within and beyond its portals.

If the site commands the south, and the approach is from that quarter also, the drive must be thrown to the east or west extreme, and, continuing well beyond the plane of the house, must circle either at the end for the entrance or be brought fully around to the north side and the entrance made there. The road must also be shielded with plantations and shrubbery.

Of course, apart from these considerations of approach and outlook, every site has its other conditions of exposure, etc. The prevailing winds in summer and winter must be studied. It may have, upon one hand, an ugly prospect, or upon another, a disagreeable neighbor; there are many points, in fact, to be carefully weighed, and many characteristics of its own calling for skill and judgment. But with its disadvantages the site must still have its good points, or it is not a site, and as the architect overcomes the former and avails of the latter, so much the greater is his credit and skill, for he will discover that in proportion as he studies and knows his site and understands its values, just in that proportion will be the success of his result.

Such is the proper house, where a site of some extent, comparatively isolated, and open to the surrounding country can be chosen.

But when the site lies in the midst of other properties already built upon, and possessing in common with them only the single outlook to the front, then the conditions of the problem require that the house shall be planned with its main approach and living-rooms alike upon this single open front. Even so, unless the lot is very narrow, a house such as is shown, with its grounds, in the plan on this page of a house at Tacoma, commends itself as still possessing, though hemmed in on three sides by residences and outbuildings, all the salient advantages of a house built in an open country.

Here the house is placed well over upon one side of the lot; the carriage-drive and walk are over against the other; the entrance-hall is at the rear of the library, with the entrance and entrance-porch at the side. In the angle of the house there is room for the turn in the drive. The grounds in front of the porch are terraced, and bordering the walk from the angle of the terrace to the entrance-porch are beds of flowers and plantations of low shrubbery. The house, with

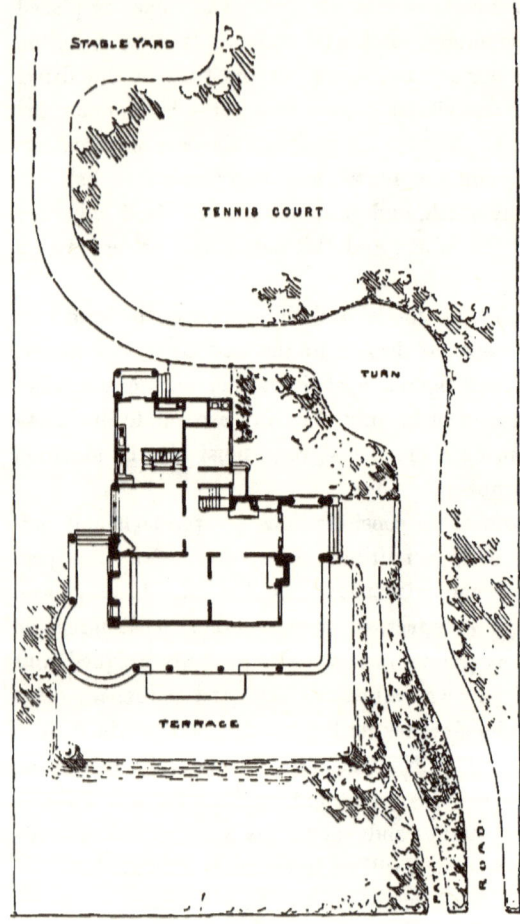

Plan of House and Grounds at Tacoma, Wash.

its porch and principal rooms thus commanded by the approach and the highway, is yet so planned and placed upon the site as to be in no way dominated by them.

A house built upon grounds on Long Island, required, from the nature of its site, a scheme of plan similar to the Tacoma house, with the difference that the entrance is at the front corner. It would be

House at Tacoma, Wash.

well suited for such a situation as the one above described is built upon.

If the site is too narrow for the drive and entrance at the side, the approach, entrance-porch, and entrance arranged at one corner of the front (as in the Long Island house), with the hall in the centre and the living porch upon the opposite corner, would give a plan meeting many of the above requirements.

But building sites laid out in nests of lots are usually narrow, and give, at best, to the sides of the houses built upon them only light and air spaces. Upon these the house is generally built across the middle of the lot, sitting back a rod or two from the road, with a walk leading from a gate in the middle of the front. Another gate and walk at one side, for tradesmen and servants, leads to the rear. For such conditions of site the problem of plan has many solutions.

A house recently built at Tuxedo would meet this problem very

House at Tuxedo, N. Y.

fairly. In this house the entrance is made at once at the centre into the hall. The porch stretches across the entire front and extends a space beyond at either side. Thus exedras are formed at the ends and give the desired living porches away from the centre and removed from the intrusion of the entrance.

Also a house at Morristown, N. J., built by Mr. Arthur Little some years since, gives an excellent solution of this "defence against the highway" idea. This house, apart from its planning and placing, is a most successful bit of shingle work, designed upon old colonial lines. [Illustration on opposite page.]

Many of the old-time houses, built upon such lots, are models of proper planning. A house in Cumberland, Md. [p. 82], is, in some respects, the most delightfully arranged home I know. It was built in the early forties from drawings by Notman. The site is upon a hill falling off sharply to the rear, with a prospect at the back of the town below, and the mountains, and narrows between them, in the distance.

The house is practically one-storied, and the charm of the plan is the directness and simplicity of its treatment.

The long axis of the house is with the length of the lot, north and south. Through the centre, from front to rear, runs the hall, fifteen feet wide and sixty feet long from door to door. Upon this hall open all the living rooms; at the front, on the right, is the parlor; on the left, the library. Beyond the parlor, on the one side, are the family bedchambers, and beyond the library, on the other, comes first a

House at Morristown, N. J.
(Arthur Little, Architect.)

guest-chamber, then the pantry and stair-hall, and the dining-room at the rear. In the roof are additional bedrooms, and in the rear basement is the kitchen, laundry, etc. Across the back of the house runs a wide porch, with a broad stair leading down to the lawn and gardens.

The quarters, or servants' building, was separate and to the left and rear of the main house. With the works of over a half century to judge it by, I do not see how a better plan could be devised for the site. Certain changes and improvements, notably in the plumbing, heating, and lighting, have been made at times by the present owner, but the body of the house is intact as Notman left it, classical in proportion, simple in outline, and refined in detail. There are numbers of inclosed lots about the suburbs of New York where just such a house could be charmingly placed.

In comparing architecturally the work of to-day with that of the various builders from colonial times up to Notman and his contemporaries, it would seem that their best work, being based strictly upon the study of classic proportions, would outlive the mass of ours. And

House at Cumberland, Md.
(Notman, Architect.)

this for the simple reason that mere novelties will not wear well. In architecture more than in any other art, the work must commend itself for some other reason than its cleverness or originality, or it will very early wear out its welcome.

"Quaint," "novel," "picturesque," are terms freely used about us to-day, and "architectural," rarely.

The old builders were *architectural*, first and always, and quaint

Cottage at Newport, R. I.
(Price, Architect.)

was perhaps as far as they ever got beyond that. It is not maintained that there is nothing in the new equal to the old, or nothing good that is not based upon some older model; or nothing good that is quaint in its effect, and both novel and picturesque as well. On the contrary, there is abundance in the new, superior in every way to the old, and architects greater and abler than the old; and much of their work is quaint and novel too, and picturesque and beautiful and original, and will last. But it will last because its motive is purely and architecturally expressed and based upon artistic principles stronger than the originality of its handling.

The old builders, though their works were at times dull and meagre and thin, were yet never undignified, never outrageous, and never forsook the idea that their work had a definite purpose and that that purpose must be expressed in it. In the Long Island, Tacoma, and Tuxedo houses it was with a thought of the old builders and their purposes that they were designed. The gambrel and deep roofs are much as they made them, and the entablature and columns are as the rules of the orders given them.

The Tacoma house [p. 79], the Armistead cottage at Newport [p. 83], and the Tuxedo house [p. 80], the writer considers a fair solution, architecturally and picturesquely, of the problem of the suburban home of moderate pretensions. Other examples are numerous; notably Mrs. Stoughton's house at Cambridge, Mass. [p. 85], one of Richardson's designs, though built of shingle in the simplest way, is in plan, mass, and treatment, one of his best works. In two instances of suburban houses by Messrs. Burnham & Root, near Chicago [pp. 87 and 88], the architects have met the problem most fairly, and show in their picturesque composition that the thought of the home was first and most important.

Of the quaint and artistic smaller cottage, two examples, most opposite in their *motif* and materials, yet both equally delightful in their architectural results, are seen in the house at Short Hills, N. J. [p. 95], built by Mr. Charles A. Rich, for himself, and the other in the suburbs of Cincinnati [p. 89], built by Mr. Trowbridge.

Of houses of greater pretensions the field is full. The Osborn house at Mamaroneck [p. 71] may be taken as an example of the best of this type. The approach is from the land side. The house is entered from a *porte-cochère* through its centre. The division of its features is in perfect sequence. All the living rooms and verandas are upon the water side; the offices and entrances upon the other. The home life is perfectly defended and protected. Architecturally the work is handled with great dignity and art. Its materials are rough granite and cedar shingles, and though born of a French *motif* it is the expo-

House at Cambridge, Mass.
(Richardson, Architect.)

nent of no style. It is moulded to the needs of its uses, and the result is a genuine American art creation, as good in itself and as honest in its purpose as any of its forerunners upon the borders of the Loire or among the hills of England.

House at Kenwood, Ill.
(Burnham & Root, Architects.)

The Megalithical houses, of which Richardson's famous Gate Lodge upon the Ames estate near Boston was perhaps the first example, appeal strongly to the original bent of the American mind. The Lodge and Keep at the main gates of Tuxedo are built of the mossy and weather-beaten rocks and bowlders found upon the slopes of the park. These are set into the walls without tool marks or fractures, and the beds and joints chocked with rock moss. The house

House at Evanston, Ill.
(Burnham & Root, Architects.)

built at Boulder Point, upon Tuxedo Lake, is a fair type of this sort. The house stands upon a cliff projecting into the lake, and its walls are carried up with the same character of rock as the cliff. The starting-courses are of the largest rocks that could be handled, and above, they grow smaller as they approach the top. Great skill is shown in the execution of the work. The stones are all selected with flat faces and fitted one against the other with great patience and care, and the result is the appearance of cyclopean masonry centuries old. In arrangement, though the house is planned to overcome the many difficulties of its site, the principle of the separation of the approaches from the living quarters, etc., is maintained.

In the details of the interior of the house of to-day, the hall, and especially its fireplace, has received much attention. The "ingle-nook" has been taken up and treated in many ways, amply and beautifully, and the impression is current that with us it is entirely a modern idea. Such is not the case. In an old house in Maryland, built long before the Revolution, the hall was of unusual size—so large, in fact, that the owner boasted that he could (and on a wager, did) turn a four-in-hand in it. On one side was an enormous fireplace, with benches built out at the sides of the jambs, and large enough to seat quite a company. This fireplace was unique. It was built of stone, broad and deep, with a heavy lintel over it; above this lintel was a niche with a separate flue from it, and here in the evening, knots of fat pine were heaped and burned, and the great hall was by this means brilliantly lighted. The old house has long since crumbled

House at Cincinnati, O
(Trowbridge, Architect.)

and rotted away, but the ruins of the old fireplace still mark the site. This house had at the time the title of being the finest one in western Maryland. Its claims to distinction rested upon the fact that the ends of the logs of which it was built were sawed off, and its roof was covered with shingles.

Viewing American houses from a standpoint of style, there is as marked a character in the artistic handling as in the planning of them.

The most distinctive national suburban house is undoubtedly the shingle house; that is, the cottage, however great or small, built of frame and covered on sides and roof with shingles, plain or ornamented as the case may be. Next in importance is the stone or brick and shingle house combined; that is, the house with the ground story of stone or brick and the upper structure of frame and shingles.

The old colonial houses cannot be considered in connection with the shingle houses of to-day. The old colonial houses were in all the best examples built upon classic lines, with a classic base for all their details and a classic feeling in their outlines.

The shingle house, while it has been recently taking a decided old colonial form, both in general and in detail, and is very distinctive in plan, began in a picturesque desire to be novel and quaint, and aimed to impress the beholder with these qualities as well as its originality above everything. That it ran riot, and is still doing so, there can be no mistake. But out of it all there is a lot of splendid work. To enumerate it or classify it is not within the scope of this article, but I am impressed with the conviction and believe in the thought that in the planning, designing, and building of the moderate-cost suburban villa of to-day, the American architect has no equal. I believe his work is well above and beyond any period of the school anywhere. Of course, I mean his best work. There is much that is bad, very bad; there have been many conditions to make it so. Vulgar and ambitious clients, uncultivated draughtsmen, who, gifted with clever manual dexterity (and our draughtsmen are getting to be very, very

House at Elberon, N. J.
(McKim, Mead, & White, Architects.)

clever as such), set up as architects; *nouveaux riches*, who gauge the beauty of their house by its cost; these and many other conditions produce inevitably their results. But when the client and his architect are in accord, the one to the manner born and the other a part of it, the results are noble and true.

Out of the abundance I select one house in particular, as the forerunner, to my mind, of the type of shingle houses that have since become so distinctively an American class. It must be now twelve or fourteen years since Mr. Victor Newcombe built his house at Elberon. It is certainly that long since I first saw it. I was driving from Sea Girt to Long Branch at the time, and, unaware of its existence, came suddenly upon it. The whole scheme, form, and treatment of the house were new to me, and I looked upon it with mingled feelings of surprise and pleasure. Mr. McKim has since done greater work, and others have done as good; for "Facilis est inventus addere," and many have profited thereby. But when I saw it first it was new and stood alone, the first of its class; and that it was true, the numbers that followed it and went beyond it soon showed. I have passed this house many times since, and to me it is as good a piece of work to-day as when I first saw it. [Illustration, page 91.]

But Mr. McKim was not the only one. Mr. Bassett Jones, fresh from the studio and influence of Norman Shaw, had built one or two lovely cottages on Staten Island. Mr. William Ralph Emerson had done likewise about Boston and at Bar Harbor. Mr. Jones's work was inspired by the Queen Anne revival then starting up in England, but so modified and adapted under his skilful treatment as to be distinctively his own. Mr. Emerson's work was more distinctive still, and went farther than either Mr. McKim's or Mr. Jones's in its individuality. While Mr. McKim, Mr. Jones, and others clothed their frame buildings with clap-boards to the height of the first story and shingled them the rest of the way up, Mr. Emerson started his shingles over the entire house at the water-table, and gained a step in repose that the other houses had not reached.

But the Queen Anne revival in England, from which all this work started, was so different in its motives, both in the use of materials and disposition of the plan, that the American cousin soon lost all

English Suburban House.
(Norman Shaw, Architect.)

family resemblance. One of the best examples of this English work, built from designs of Norman Shaw, is shown in the above illustration of an English suburban house. It is delightful in composition, is essentially a home, and meets exactly the English idea of one; raise it from the ground, put a veranda around it, and transplant it to New York, and its congruity is destroyed.

Under such conditions and aided in his work by the increasing knowledge and higher cultivation of our intelligent people in all matters pertaining to art, the American architect of to-day finds his great opportunity to found an American style. That the American country-

House at Short Hills, N. J.
(Rich, Architect.)

house has become distinctive in becoming suited to our economies and habits of life is clear. Our wants call for new forms in plan and masses ; our materials for new lines and textures in elevations ; and with our national inventiveness fostered by the problem, our work becomes more and more national. All these conditions demand original thought and hard study ; and bending the mind and talents to answering them must produce distinctive results.

The feeling of the old may survive, but the style of the prototype has been bent to the homes we live in, and in bending yields to a new form. The new form, begun in a friendly school, will often borrow from a sympathetic type, and the result, while neither of the two, yet is true to both ; true to its new conditions and good withal. And so the American architect is passing into his incipient Renaissance, copying less from the masters he has studied and reveres, and dropping the word style from his practice. How that word rises up ; a frowning spectre to some, a safeguard to many! How can the American practitioner be true to it? Will his client have a replica from Italy, from France, or even from England? Will he build and live in a Scotch fastness, with high, draughty halls, ill lit from narrow windows, flood his moat, haul up his bridge, and lower his portcullis with the chiming of the vesper bells? Will he plant his roof-tree upon the walls of a French *manoir*, give up his ground floor to carriage-drive and flunkies' quarters and live above stairs? Will he give up his shady porches, his wide verandas, his broad piazzas, and take the style he asks for in the literal truth of its examples? There are none of these, as he knows and needs them, in the great schools from which he would borrow a name for his cottage. True, there are verandas in Italy, and *loggias*, too, in both Italy and France that lend ideas—and beautifully they have been used. But American life could not thrive —could not exist, indeed—housed in any of the buildings upon which these are found. American country life has marked out its current— broad, clear, well defined. It has its source in a thousand well-springs deep down in the national character. Hampered with no traditions, with a quick perception of his wants, an innate love of the beautiful, independent and practical, the American must inevitably show his national traits in his home. Scattered apart or grouped together, upon the hills, in valleys, and along the streams that wander through them to the ocean, or perched upon the bluffs and beaches that mark its boundaries, for encircling miles about our great cities, have sprung up, and are still rising, the true homes of the American of to-day. From them and to them a great tide ebbs and flows, and pours over the ferries, by the cars, and along the great water-ways every day. Never ceasing, this torrent pours in and pours out, stronger and greater year by year, giving to the life of the day one of its most distinctive features. In all the rush, in the marvellous phases that have marked the growth and progress of our wonderful epoch, there is nothing so impressive in the city's life as this daily coming and going throng. It is a vivid expression of that American trait which inspires every man, no matter how subordinate his position in the business world, to assert his individuality and independence by owning a home which is the outgrowth of his special tastes and needs. Amid the pretences and shams of which American life is often accused, this at least has the instinct of truth, and an honest purpose.

THE COUNTRY HOUSE

By DONALD G. MITCHELL

FIRST of all, in broaching the topic assigned me, I must venture upon a little preliminary talk about what is really meant by the term Country House. There are those in these times who would persuade us that all country houses—as implying country homes—are going clean out of date. It was only a few weeks back that I fell upon the reading of a three-column article in a great metropolitan journal, which set forth the notion that no sensible, well-cultured person ought in future to entertain any purpose of living in the country, or of going there in any domiciliary way, except for a brief outing in the heats of summer; and this "able" writer blew such a cloud of logical dust in one's eyes as caused the trees and the fields to take on a blurred look, and made an old-fashioned man's love for them seem quite disreputable.

Nevertheless, I count it not altogether presumptuous to suppose, and even confidently to believe, that people of considerable parts will continue to establish themselves and their homes in the country, and to wrestle with its disadvantages, through longer or shorter series of years.

It is not of those suburban dwellers that I speak now, who come to the country for their sleepings and their Sundays, but whose interests and engagements hold all their energies to task-work between the walls of city houses. I can understand how these people, who are shot in grooves back and forth between their city working-places and those outside harbors where they anchor at nightfall, should equip these harbors of refuge with a great many of the coquetries of architecture, and lavish upon them much goodly spoil of horticulture; but it is not of these suburban rests (I had almost said roosts) that I am to speak, but rather of those houses, inland, which make more determinate homes, and which involve an acquaintance with the summer noonings as well as the summer nights.

Again, it is needful to exclude from present discussion those architectural retreats of the mountains, or by the shore, which are only known to the holders, and only enjoyed during August and September heats; and so—whatever dances may enliven them, or whatever dinners or guests make them gay—never get the qualities of a country family homestead.

I know very many of these summering places are, in these latter years, specially taking on an importance and a fulness of equipment that may even match the city homes of their owners; but if they get every autumn a double fastening of the cupboards, and a padlocking of the gates, and such dispersion of all servitors as forbids any blue pennon drifting from the chimney-tops in winter, and any welcoming bound of the house-dog (if the owner pays visit), they belong only to that category of half-homes with which we are not now concerned. Among the qualities which mark and differentiate the country house and home, as we understand it, may be counted this ever-ready openness—fires that do not go out, portraits of our grandfathers and mothers (if we have them) upon the wall, and gardens that get their belaboring with the spade as surely as every spring comes. A man may indeed divide his honors, if he have enough, and, like Queen Victoria, equip one home with Tudor ancestors, and sanctify another with the Hanoverian portraits; but barred gates and a summer rioting of weeds on house-paths make a desertion in which a sturdy home sentiment, that ought to lurk in all country houses, cannot grow.

Again, it does not appear to me that the good countryish qualities of house and home are to be measured exactly by distance from cities.

Garden sanctities and charms may thrive in the very shadow of town steeples; and I can imagine that the wiser ones of the Fox family took infinite satisfaction in the pretty bosky covers of Holland House long after the tide of London brick and mortar flowed clamorously around its garden walls. Many of the most engaging types of our American country houses were planted on roads that became the

Rock Hall, near Rockaway, Long Island.

streets of bustling towns or of cities. I recall in this connection that old Longworth homestead which for so many years held its dignified rural quietudes of trees and garden in the midst of the noisy growth of Cincinnati; again, there is the John Bartram house, on the Schuylkill, retaining its country charms of vines and flowers—its birds even —long after city sounds had drowned their songs. I recall also many a quiet old town along the shores of Long Island Sound, or of the Connecticut River, where broad-faced trim houses of a colonial type, with airy halls and balustrades upon their roofs, are still full of a rural invitingness which is made good by their great gardens in the rear, and by their alleys of boxwood in the front. The interjection on the

Example of Old House in Interior of Connecticut.

village street of butcher shops and of telegraph offices does not kill the high country qualities of such homes.

Having thus by this prefatory process of exclusion put out of present range the watering-place houses and those suburban retreats from which occupants change from year to year, we narrow our outlook to those houses, of large or small importance, which make permanent homes, and rally best one's rural instincts. There was no lack of these in our early times. Satan had not set up his alluring city sign-boards so thickly in those days. There are lingerers from that old date to be seen everywhere in our Eastern and Middle States. Who does not know those little, one-story, unpainted, cube-shaped, wooden houses scattered all along New England shores, from Marblehead to Guilford, on sandy knolls, on the flank of hills—any site was good, if a woodchuck could dig his hole there without being drowned out in storms; the big stone chimney in the middle, cumbrous and mighty with its crude masonry, gave space abreast of it for front " entry " way; on one side a bedroom, on the other the " keeping " room, with a musty smell about it; and behind the chimney the great common room, kitchen, what-not, with its pantry at one end, and possible cramped stair to a loft under the " half-pitch " roof where a helper in harvesting, and—by proper partitioning—girls in their teens, might get a "shake-down " of straw mattress.

There are lordly men in our history, growing in honors year by year, who have had their rearing in such quarters. The shape was sensible, because it was of the simplest, and met all the necessities of the case (can there be a better rule in any architecture?). The cover-

Rhode Island and Connecticut Shore House.

ing was of riven shingles, which in the progress of years and storms gave us that delightful tint of weather-worn wood, which the painters cannot match, nor, I am afraid, the engravers.

Following upon the simplest type came the lift of the roof into that gambrel shape which was token of more room and consequence, and which—so far as my observation has reached—seems to have developed specially on the immediate seaboard; perhaps because its lines were more ship-shape and gave to the roof a faint semblance to a vessel's bottom [p. 103]. A Dutch modification of this form is to be found on Long Island and in New Jersey; while a modernization of the same—with fantastic array of bowlder work—is to be seen in the "Falmouth" cottage [p. 105]. To the original type there came in the early days a jutting out rearward of pantries, milk-rooms, summer-kitchens, spare bedrooms, which involved a stretch of roof: and of this stretch of roof was very likely legitimately begotten that form of homestead so well known along all the older-settled portions of the valley of the Connecticut, with long sloping roof in the rear, and narrower roof covering the two stories in the front. And this was eminently a com-

Specimen of Early Dutch Architecture, Long Island, N. Y.

mon-sense type of house, giving recognition to the fact, that though a man might need two stories in front, a single one would serve him in the rear; demonstrating also the fact that uniformity of roof and of roof-pitch on both sides were not essential to good effect [p. 106]. Indeed this association of long roof slope and other forms is showing itself with great piquancy in many modern country houses.

As for interior arrangements, there was here a great central stack

Residence of Joseph Hopkins Smith, Falmouth, Me.
(John Calvin Stevens, Architect.)

of chimneys, showing good gray gneiss or sandstone at the tops; the stairs zigzagged up abreast of it before the front door, giving space for a table or a cupboard under them; right and left, two front rooms—the southerly one having, most times, door opening upon yard or garden—and in the rear the great kitchen, possibly flanked by back-stairs opening on the wainscot, and certainly with a great wealth of closets. Nay, there was hardly one of them, of whatever proportions, but came ultimately to have its extension hipped upon the northern angle, for further exploitation of the home laboratory—for milk, wood, shelter over the well, and for making grateful lee at the back entrance against fierce "Northers." And there was a delightful honesty in this architectural confession of small home wants not to be found in many modern houses. In our electric age there is disposition to ignore such

Characteristic New England House, especially in towns along the Connecticut River.

needs and to do away with "backdoors;" hence comes that overnicety in country-house surroundings, amid which a visitor must look long and drearily for a place where he can knock the ashes from his pipe.

Thereafter came swiftly, abundant modifications of this form: an overjutting of second story, and again of the loft floor, with supporting beams, making crude machicolations, types of which abound in the Farmington (Conn.) Valley. The Avery house built in 1656, a few miles eastward of New London, and still stanch in its timbers, is notable for its quaintness and for having sheltered eight successive generations of the same family. Some thirty years after its erection the proprietor bought a condemned church in a near town and spliced it upon his homestead; and there, in Revolutionary times, when the

Avery head of the house had become an urgent "Separatist," public psalm-singing and preaching were heard again. Another curious agglomeration of house roofs, and addenda of even date, but of more importance, is that of the famous Wentworth mansion at Little Harbor. The old "Fairbanks" homestead at Dedham may be named in this connection [p. 108].

When the central stack of chimneys was divided—increased size of fortune or family demanding more fires—there came about the long central hall dividing the house, through which in August came that refreshing play of the winds which so many old people remember with

Old House of Peter Avery, Pequonnoc, Conn., built in 1656.

joy. Many early houses with two gaunt gray chimneys show stairways cloven into the side-walls of the hall, and closed in by doors; then came the open balusters and the half climb to a great landing, set

Fairbanks House at Dedham, Mass., built in 1636.

off with round-topped window at the end of the hall; and as this hall gained in width and importance, heavy wooden cornices adorned it, a great archway divided it, oaken panelwork grew upon the side-walls, and a great flood of light from the big window on the landing showed marvellous landscapes from the Dutch paper-hangers between the wainscot and cornice. Or maybe there was some quiet monotone of color upon the walls, on which hung family portraits by Copley, or Smybert, or the Earles, with a tall clock ticking on the stair-landing or within the archway: very cold straits of passage in winter these great halls made between the blazing firesides in the rooms flanking them, till Nott's stoves and the cellar furnaces came in; but in summer what delightful affluence of breezes, with their flavors of lilies or of locust bloom!

To this fashion of houses belong those so-called colonial mansions which give dignity to so many outlying towns around Massachusetts Bay; great pilasters, may be, at their angles, and marking the interior partitions; *frontons* of classic treatment, with central ornamented window; balustrades; perhaps some lifted room at the apex of the hipped roof (as in the Fisher house of Dorchester); possibly a labored cutting of the wooden angles into the semblance of stone quoins (as in the Deming House, of Colchester). A great many of these features were repeated in country houses that grew up along the heights of New York Island—among them the Apthorp mansion, now made

Johnson Hall, Johnstown, N. Y., built in 1764 by Sir William Johnson.

dreary by neglect. Of a less imposing house in the same region, I come upon this pleasant mention in an old letter * of the time, from

* Brought to light in that agreeable reservoir of colonial data, the *Pennsylvania Magazine of History*.

Mrs. Thomson, wife of the Secretary of Congress (1786). She is commending a rich widow, with £10,000 in her own right, to a gentleman friend in Philadelphia. She says: " Her house is pleasantly situated; the front has a view of the North River, and from the back you can see the East River. The house is one story high, with attick chambers; there is a Piazza all round the dwelling; the widow is cheerful and comely—inclines to be Plump."

Farther up the Hudson (Yonkers) was that interesting Phillipse manor-house, now—if standing at all—given over to civic uses; again, and specially noticeable as exhibiting the classic architectural fervors of the latter half of the last century was the Montgomery Place, at Barrytown, still maintaining its dignities amid its encompassing wood. The well-known Patroon house, of Albany (of latter part of seventeenth century), was less classic, but palatial in extent, and understood to repeat the features of the Dutch homestead of the Van Rensselaers in Holland. Along that valley of the Mohawk—are still standing many notable country houses of the last century; among them, the home of Sir William Johnson (near to Johnstown), with central round-topped window setting off its upper story, hipped roof, and its two flanking buildings, standing apart for offices and bachelor quarters [p. 109]; the old Herkimer house, where the hero of Oriskany died, is yet inhabited; and another noble homestead, simple, grand, and stately (built by Jan Linklaen, in the last century), maintains its dignity and its air of high hospitalities amid the leafy charms of Cazenovia [p. 111].

Farther westward, in the valley of the Genesee, widely known for its beauty and its fertilities, there came as settler, in the closing years of the last century, a Connecticut man (from Durham), who had a keen eye for good land and for good landscape, and who before his death (1844) made the Wadsworth estate known for its great reach, and its abounding productiveness; and made himself known by quiet and large philanthropies. The homestead that grew up there under the fostering care of a son—who found an honored death at the head of his brigade in the battle of the Wilderness—is more essentially a

Linklaen House (eighteenth century). Cazenovia, N. Y.
(Built by Jan Linklaen, agent of the Dutch Government.)

country home than the others we have brought to view. It is situated upon a slope of those gently rising, broad-surfaced hills from which there is wide valley outlook over groups of forest trees and fertile meadows. It is not specially noticeable for its architectural lines, except that a great profusion of them, in shape of oriels, gables, porches, chimneys, give promise of comfort; the stretch of fields and of trees make the divorce from city and suburban things complete. Even a meeting of the hounds there does not tempt the derisive smile which is provoked by the artificialities of a "hunt" at Newport [pp. 119 and 121].

Reverting again to earlier phases of American country life, I am tempted to speak of that great estate which, in pre-Revolutionary days, William Alexander—known as Lord Stirling—equipped, at prodigious cost, near to Basking Ridge, in New Jersey. There was a huge mansion, with imposing drawing-room and banqueting-hall, with stuccoed ceiling; a long array of offices, with coach-houses, bake-houses, brew-houses; all these skirting a paved quadrangle, and showing gilded vanes disporting over the cupolas. Judge Jones, the loyalist and historian (who had himself a great country house near South Bay, L. I., still held by the Floyd-Joneses), says that Stirling "cut a splendid figure, having brought with him from England horses, carriages, a coachman, valet, butler, cook, steward, hairdresser, and a mistress." This Lord Stirling, however, fought bravely on the patriot side, and held Washington's esteem; but the war, his absence, and lack of trading shrewdness, brought his fortune to wreck, and before the end of the century the Basking Ridge establishment was in ruins. All the aspects of this, in its palmy days, and its management, must have been rather foreign than American. The same is also true of the country estate near Bordentown, one while occupied and improved by Joseph Bonaparte.

Another New Jersey country establishment of a more strictly American type, and still showing its hugely timbered barns of American pattern, is the so-called Bingham House in Oceanic. At a dance in its great banqueting-hall it is said that the beautiful Miss Bingham lost her heart—carrying therewith a great slice of her father's landed estate—to Lord Ashburton. The ground plan shows lack of all lesser

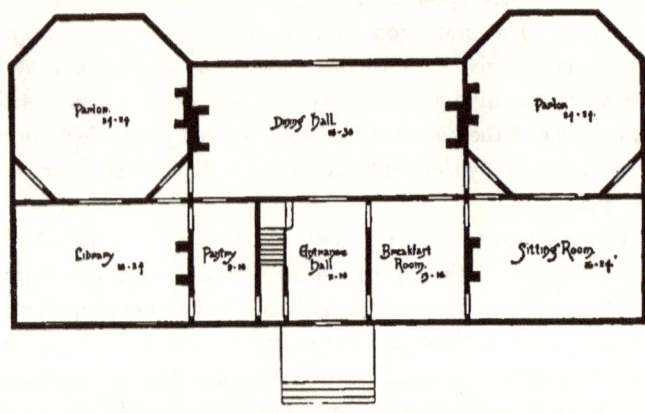

Plan of Bingham House at Oceanic, N. J., owned by Dr. Ehrick Parmly.

offices, which were established in octagonal buildings flanking the main house, but slightly in the rear, and connected with it, originally, by corridors. Magnificent trees still belong to the site, and a great lawn (cut athwart by a *ha-ha*, beyond which cattle feed) sweeps from its front to a shore where some leafless remnants of old forest bear up ospreys' nests, and the ocean beats and thunders.

The great simplicity of the ground floor, with no kitchen involvements, was characteristic of most Southern country homes, to which dinners came in steaming from without. The Stratford (Lee) house, with its low roofs and curiously grouped chimneys, is an example of this, dating from about the middle of the last century [p. 115]. Another notable Virginia house, Mount Vernon, all the world knows of ; and the tall, massive colonnade supporting the extension of its long roof had its *replicas* in climates not so well suited to such defence against the sunbeams. Thus General Huntington—Washington's Collector of Customs in New London—built there a commodious house, upon a gentle height, then outside the town, with massive brick columns of quaint form supporting the overreach of roof upon three sides. It has been well preserved, save that within a few years a bay window and an oriel of modern demonstrative carpentry has been thrust across the Mount Vernon extension of roof, showing how bumptious common-sensical notions about light and air will cut clean through and destroy the charms of traditionary form.

Early country houses in lower Virginia, between the York and James Rivers, were built more after accredited English forms, and the materials for them were largely imported. The same is true of early

Stratford House, Westmoreland County, Va.
(Built in the eighteenth century, of brick sent over from England, for Colonel Thomas Lee, great-grandfather of General Robert E. Lee. This house is the birthplace of General Lee.)

houses in South Carolina; and there are roof-tiles covering outbuildings and stables in Charleston, still in good condition, which were brought, more than a century ago, from Holland. So were the bricks and Portland stone which went to the making of the Alston house (known for its vaulted drawing-room), and to the walls that hemmed in the great garden where it was planted. The material in Drayton Hall, built in the middle of the last century (1747), and almost the only important homestead along the Ashley River which escaped the scathing times of the war, is also of British origin. It is without cellar, and for sanitary reasons—like most country houses in the lower Carolinas—is lifted high above the ground, and amid a lusty overgrowth of vines and shrubs shows a dignified front and a hospitable amplitude.

The inland "up-country" homesteads—even of those who planted largely—were generally of much more modest pretentions, the original and humblest type being the log-house—perhaps doubled, with an airy, roofed corridor between the couple. The coupling might run

Mantel in the Wister House, Germantown, Pa.

Chew House, Germantown, Pa.

to three or four; and these, when built with care, and weatherboarded and painted—with roofs stretching over into long verandas—with a near whitewashed group of servants' quarters, and here and there a guest's cottage, or that of the doctor or of the chaplain, upon a neighboring wooded knoll—were not without their invitingness and importance. Instances of extraordinary expenditure upon some of the upland places were not unknown. Thus the late Governor Manning built, and equipped luxuriously, a great establishment, "Milford," in central South Carolina. It was a grand surprise for a visitor—after toiling through silent stretches of pine woods—to come upon a great *fronton* of imposing Greek columns, ponderous doors of rosewood, lofty frescoed ceilings, silken bell-pulls, and Parisian *bric-à-brac*. Yet the dreaded "country fever" compelled the abandonment of all this, by both master and guest, so soon as the May sun smote hotly the spongy surface of the near cypress swamps.

Country houses in the Southwest, upon the river banks above New Orleans, formed a type of their own—great verandas with blooming things scrambling over them making part; so did the magnolias and pecan-trees. There was a large grouping of 'outside offices—sometimes also of school and chapel, in connection with neatly organized quarters—which together made a little hamlet.

The English quadrangle system of country-house establishments never came to great vogue in America. It belonged to a mediævalism that has left its musty odors only about some of our educational buildings. Even the "walling in" cumbrously of courts or gardens is rarely seen. Our hot suns of summer do not favor the use of such protection; wall-fruit is not the success here that it is in England; even in the case of open espaliers (always associated with old British country houses) there is need for keeping a leafier growth than is admissible under the leaden skies of the Old Country.

There must be opportunity for some quite new and rare development of rural buildings under the conditions belonging to life on the great ranches of Colorado and California. The family of the redwoods furnishes rare material, if the old adobe be not brought to noble uses; and no setting for whatever roofs, cupolas, cattle-pens, barracks, olive-presses, can be imagined finer than the snow-tipped mountains of Colorado, or the verdurous ones of southern California.

The question of site for a country home, is an important one, East or West; and involves other and quite different conditions from those to be considered on a suburban street. The vagaries of our climate within the last half dozen years have somewhat disturbed the old notions about shelter from northwesters; but I think there will be general agreement that the flank of a hill is better for site than the extreme summit; and the opinion is well supported that a southwestern exposure (and slope for ground) is, of all, the best, and cheeriest, and kindliest, whether for house or gardens. The perfect drainage which

Wadsworth Homestead in the Genesee Valley, Western New York.

every wise man will seek for in a country house, is, of course, more easily secured by elevated site ; and the old closed cesspool is giving way to one which shall serve as the distributing reservoir for a system of subsurface tiling. The distribution may be secured at short periods by the action of a siphon, or by flushing the reservoir from the rain conduits.

Of the material for the construction of a country house there are divers opinions and practices ; but there is a growing (and wise) disposition to use homely material, nearest at hand, if sound and effective. The old bugbear that stones made a damp house is disproved by those who build, with such "furring off" of inner walls as insures dryness as well as warmth in winter, and best protection of all against fierce sunbeats.

Staircase in Wadsworth House, Geneseo.

If house walls are not wholly of stone, multitudes show that bold use of it in the ground-story which has gone perhaps to make it too popular ; by this I mean that its opportunities tempt finical littlenesses of treatment. I have seen this effect by use of oversmall stones, perhaps, of regularly recurring sizes, nestled together like child's work; and again by undue care to give all stones the same form, or same lack of form; both these methods being bad, and defeating that sensible purpose—simple as it is sensible—to make a stanch wall, wholly sufficient, and without those affectations of *petit-maître*-ism, in quality or tone, which defeat every aim of honesty and all heroic simplicities. An exaggerated rudeness—specially in use of rude material—is as bad as an exaggerated finesse; and is it not an overstrain of plain bowlder work to lay it up in columns with Pelasgic hugeness for the support of a veranda, or mere umbrage roof of whatever sort?

Not least among the advantages of this use of stone for the ground story is its invitingness for vine growth. I know there are some sticklers for the old notion that such growth promotes dampness; but the shelter of the leaves, and the evaporation from them of such moisture as the little rootlets have taken up from the stone and mortar go far to disprove the old belief, if long and actual test had not shown contrary result.

Shingles have been latterly put to greatly increased uses in covering walls as well as roofs of country houses, and with the variety of good stains now available have excellent effect; but it is a questionable, and, architecturally, indefensible use which puts them to the cover of supporting columns to a porch, or to the dressing of an arch in carpentry. Among the stains that have come into use appears a very clever counterfeit (as respects color) of those delicate gray-green lichens which age puts upon many old houses; but shall an honest country home carry even so pretty a falsehood as this upon its roof?

Of course the selection of material for country building will be largely governed by the general outline and style; those imposing, dignified, half classic, colonial houses, of which we spoke, and which have some rare qualities for comfort, would not admit of a jumble of stones and timber, or of any tricks for the picturesque; yet that old Connecticut-River type of a long slope in the rear roof, and of over-

Hyde Hall, Cooperstown, N. Y.

reach, with show of supporting timbers of the upper floor, would sit very well upon a good honest ground story of stone-work, incorporated with some massive chimneys piling up to the height of the ridge. And that upper story could be happily married to the ground by a heavy timber porch at its door, with its inviting seats; or, if need were, some more closely wrought lee against northers for the visitor in waiting. Every country house demands a porch of some sort; dignity and hospitality both demand it; but the *porte-cochère* is of more doubtful necessity; it may be made to take abundance of picturesque

Lodge Gate, Hyde Hall.

attitudes indeed, but is very apt—save under quite exceptional treatment—to put unwelcome shadows and gloom about an entrance, suggestive of lingering damp at the step, or of long unmelting annoyances of ice. Cheer, warmth, sunshine ought to be flung with full hands about the grand and chiefest opening to a home. 'Twere well, therefore, to relegate this coach sheltering (and a country coach ought to brave a good deal of honest, hard weather) to a secondary and side door, where the shadows of its long overreach will not tell harmfully.

As for the windows of a country house, the demand should be for largeness, and, again—largeness; indeed some corridor with walls of glass is not a bad accompaniment for a flank or angle. Our sanitarians are getting, at last, to understand the glory and the goodness of a winter's sunshine, and that it is no way needful to journey to the tropics for it. Whether the large glazing which will insure a good sun-bath can be associated with good flower-growth is more doubtful; succulent plants, at least, for their fullest growth require a humidity of air not good for human wants; but I have seen one of the great piazzas flanking a country house of the Revolutionary type, which, having taken on its winter (movable) wall of glazing, giving shelter to certain tough bits of green—such as a rampant ivy, or a group of aspedistas, or some tall fellow of the palm family in his tub—make an uncommonly welcome place for an after-dinner smoke, or a booklet (in the hammock), or an idle listening to the canary which swung out of Tabby's reach, and sung the snows to shame.

What now shall be said of the hall of a country house, except that it should make good the welcome of the porch and of the sunny windows and of the chimney-tops? For this it should never be cramped: that is a pinch at the very vitals of a home. And yet fair proportions must be guarded: it offers tempting place for an architect to lavish his skill; but neither its extent nor appointments should dwarf the house; as if a host were to spend his forces in an unctuous shaking of hands, without any larder to back up his welcome!

Shall there be fireplace in the hall? If never to be used, and set there—in however piquant dress of oak and brazen trappings—only as a symbol of a warmth which never shows tongue of flame, emphatically no. Doubtful even if the lighting only on far apart festal days could justify it; but if the logs are to glow or smoulder on that altar (as weather may bid) from the ides of November to those of April, or if its flames are to light the mornings of a belated spring, or warm the nightfalls of a frosty October, it is an unmatchable glory of a country house; unless indeed the rollicking blaze play of a library fire or of a breakfast-room matches it. A country house without its fireplaces, or something with a blaze in them, is like a man groping for treasure with eyes put out. As for smoky chimneys, there is no reasonable

House of Edward Livingston, Lenox, Mass.
(Rotch & Tilden, Architects.)

excuse for them; the main points are a narrow throat, and a good cushioning of air behind it for any sudden down draught: to this end a slant forward of the rear wall is best, and a good splaying of the jambs.

Of course there may be exterior reasons for bad draught—in presence of a near overtopping building, or dense wood, or sudden rise of hill—which causes of trouble are oftenest circumvented by an embranchment of chimney-tops, as pleasantly explained and justified by M. Viollet le Duc, in his agreeable "Story of a House."

Next, stairs. To many a poor woman who has toiled a half life out upon an eight-inch "rise" of stair, a lessening of the height by two inches (six and one-eighth inches is best) will seem like putting step on the road to Beulah. A steep stair everywhere, and everyhow —except in a ship's steerage—is an offence and a blight and a curse. But for an easy, hospitable, broad, cheery, inviting stairway flanking a country hall, or engrossing one end of it, or dominating it by a great swing of its galleries or landing, what a noble chance is given to the architect! What woody rioting there may be in balusters—in screens lifting up to the support of great beams in the ceiling, in arches disguising the changing levels, in flashes from mosaic windows, pouring glories on the floor! We might fill our pages with pretty illustrations thereanent; but from all we should very likely come back to a quickened love for those old simplicities which associate perfect ease with severest of lines.

As for collocation of rooms in country houses, there is happily no occasion for all those Chinese puzzlings and dove-tailings of parts which city architects find it needful to study. There is, or should be, space to thrust out a room or a bay or an L, where we need it; and as for the sun, windows may be set to welcome it. The morning sun, by all means, should come to the family room, to the children's room, and to the breakfast-room; as for the afternoon sun, let it strike where it will. In all our latitudes, south or north, the southwest angle of a house is, I think, the treasured angle—most to be coveted for chambers, for work-room, for (if it must be) sick-room. The sun stays there longest; the blues vanish fastest.

The wants of children, too, must not be left out of sight, unless we determine to legislate them away, and make Mr. Malthus our saint. There's no in-door romping-ground for a child like a great garret, with dormers to let in sunlight like a deluge. The quaint, big old houses we have shown, had them; and a healthy child, without chance for

McAlpin House, Sing Sing, N. Y.
(Hapgood, Architect.)

rainy-day forays in such, must grow up with a large domestic element of its nature undeveloped. Home ties of those young folk grapple to a bare roof-tree in the top of the house very clingingly. And if country life is not to be subverted altogether, and turned adrift on the wastes of cities, it must be the clinging child-love, wakening in manhood, and re-awakening in age, which is to insure and ennoble its best development.

By the same ruling there must be out-of-door regalement and comforters of the child-age. "Out-of-doors" is a very large part of a well-balanced country house; this is an Irishism, maybe; but it is a wholesome one to consider and act upon. "Out-of-doors" in cities does not tie to the dwelling; it lacks privacy; it lacks consecration; it is every man's; and so no man's. There should be tennis-ground; there should be coasting hill; there should be skating-pond, snow forts, and fortresses of stone; cabins—for cooking—for picnicing, for learning the ductilities that belong to the offices of hostess. *Home* is the word; to give great quickening sense to it, to ennoble it, to endear it, to justify it; this is, or ought to be, the aim where roof-trees are planted in the open of God's country. One of the greatest of lacks, as appears to me, in the pretty Bellamy programmes of social fixtures, is that they disjoint and fling apart all old and relishable ideas of home, leaving no place for their development. Such schemes legislate away need for it: for, what is home without its teapot singing on the hearth, without its rallying-place at the fireside for family seclusion; without its "table-round," where books, games, singing, talk—unhampered by over-critical ears—fill up the eventide; without, maybe, its household mishaps of kitchen or larder, bewraying the management and compelling virtues of self-denial—of gracious reticence—of quiet, brave reconcilement with the accidents of life?

Gardens, too; what is your country house without a garden? And by garden I mean all those encompassing or outlying things of green which need coaxing, and training, and loving, for their development. There need be no great trail of such—no sheltering quadrangular courts. But surely no mistress can wear so beautiful and so cheap an adornment as a flower. Timid ones need not be frightened with bugbear stories of how B—— raises tomatoes at cost of a dollar each, and his chrysanthemums at cost of his wife's ostrich plumes. A little care and sympathy, and two hours of a morning will do the needful. There is no need for any rioting with moneys; and a flower that blooms responsive to one's training and care carries double perfume; and the fruit a man picks from his own "graffing" has subtle flavors that trace back through all the gardens in books.

I do not believe a man can be proper æsthetic master of what belongs to a country house—to its amplitudes or proportions, or harmonies (*pace*, Mr. Architect)—except he see his way to them through alleys of green. Great reach and tale of acres upon acres are not essential. I do not know but the rural instincts are more deeply and certainly stirred by some old half-country half-town house, where the village road brings its *carryall* in shower-time-nearness to the door. I have such an one very plainly in my mind's eye, as I write; the low ceilings (which would make modern fine builders stand aghast), couple cosily with the old-time chairs ; the sun is shining through vases that carry dainty blossoms in southern windows ; the great sweep of fifty-year-old Norway spruces (which some livers by the sea opinionate can never become great, lusty trees), put their dark fringes of boughs wooingly to the shaven green ; the little terraced bit of old garden (a Brobdignag handkerchief would cover it), shows an ancient shaky trellis for a big-leaved vine (is it the "Dutchman's Pipe"?) ; old-time herbaceous flowers, such as the Fraxinella, white and red, are there ; so are lilies of the valley, and tall blue-bells gone astray in grass, and giving out perfume like the breath of babes ; masses of moss-pink, too, spreading rosy bloom, and hedges of box, with strange mystic scent from their stirred leaves—odors of dead years.

It is not long ago that I came upon record—in the pleasant *London Garden*—of a Gloucestershire parson, who wrote with unction and zeal and knowledge of his miniature vicarage ground, and of his rockwork. "Six feet by eight, with twenty-one different species of plants growing in it, and all thriving ;" and he goes on to detail other horticultural triumphs, pleasant, fine, and positive, though only himself and a "fag of all work" keep the exterior machinery of the modest country home he lived in on the move and on the make. Not money-making, to be sure ; that reckoning were a dishonest way of estimating the subtle pleasures of those who, like the Gloucestershire parson, enwrap themselves—spring-time and autumn—in the delights of a rural home. That figure of the factotum, too, has its country sufficiencies, and touches of familiar regalement for a good many of us

House of Lyman Josephs, Newport, R. I.

who have conspired with sympathetic architects for a home in the country : 'tis not a de Coverley picture, this factotum ; lean and slight ; cocking his eye with a knowing upturn to read all promises of weather ; not pinning his beliefs to newspaper probabilities ; scanning the roses, and the beans, and the carrots, with a serener faith in their growing powers than comes of books ; doubled-up, odd whiles, with agues ; but slouching to his rainy-day plantings under a great cover of draggled clothes ; too old to be taught ; crowding down your finer knowledges with Solomon-like sayings, and enforcing their wisdom with a sharp catarrhal discharge between thumb and forefinger ; honest as the day, and with a humorsome joy shimmering in his face when he sees long-doubted seeds of his saving breaking the ground, and stays his hoe for a new lighting of his brier pipe ; old and rheumatic, but finding compensation in his mastery of the ground and the seasons.

If I were to search in a wide New England neighborhood for one who enjoyed most, and made the most of a country home—because of its countryish elements—I do not think I should consider the great show places ; but the rather some modest house, half sunk upon a hillside ; its basement windows fronting the morning ; greensward coming to the door ; the conservatory a window shelf ; every slip of a new plant cherished ; every spring some modest extension of the flower-patch ; a little orchard flanking and protecting the garden where the mistress walks proudly among her nasturtiums and her scarlet beans, and cares as tenderly for every shrub and blooming thing as for the kittens that frolic at the door.

These addenda, these surroundings, are to be considered in any estimate of the forms which a country house should take, and for the conditions which it should most wisely fulfil. No country house which does not mate with "all-round" country laws can be architecturally good. Strip the vines and the grouped masses of foliage from that old Bartram house, of which we spoke in an earlier page, and there is left only a coarse, bare hulk of wall. Shear away those piles of foliage—

those bristling points of firs which approach and environ it, and—by proper occasions of retreat—leave embayments of sunny turf around the great Genesee house, which was figured upon an earlier page, and we should fatally misjudge it. That modest country house—so well known—of Sunnyside, which was for so long, and worthily, a quickener of rural instincts, owes no small proportion of its charm to its *entourage* of foliage and the great vine that enwraps its principal outbuilding. Modest as it is, and inexpensive in its details, it is still a good exemplar of what may be done with homely material. Mr. Irving certainly had the rural instincts strongly developed; long, and very tenderly that image of Wolfert's Roost (his charming home) lay near to his thought, and brooded there through years of Continental travel—brooded there always till the trees were planted, the duck-pond set to its flow, and the old Dutch weather-vane put to its spinning over the crow-foot gable that rose above his southern porch. The dogs, the kittens, the doves, the cows, even the pigs of his country home, were all companionable with him; and he loved the things of the garden: not the flowers only, and the little trap of a green-house he had improvised in a corner, but the trim rows of vegetables as well. With what a rare gusto (if I may play the reporter upon the weaknesses of a host) he looked upon the yellowing melons, bathing in the sunshine, and on the purple glories of the egg-plants! "Not *like* them! (with a wondering lift of the eyebrows) why, a broiled slice of one is richer than a rasher of bacon."

SMALL COUNTRY PLACES

By SAMUEL PARSONS, Jr.

A FRIEND once asked me for advice in relation to a place he had just inherited. He was one of those men who always set out and do the thing they want to do, and then ask for advice when it is too late. Unsuspicious of the condition of affairs, I held forth at length on the questions of site and other equally important considerations connected with a small country place.

Time passed and I received a pressing invitation to spend Sunday with him. Of course, on reaching the place, I naturally hoped to see some results of the advice so freely and earnestly given, for I had conceived a high regard for my friend, and did not want to see him go wrong and waste his money. To my surprise, I came upon a conspicuous example of most of the errors I had warned him to avoid. He divined something of the thoughts that must naturally pass through my mind, and began to explain that he had done most of this work before he spoke to me. Indeed, he waxed earnest and explained to me carefully how the architectural style of his house, old colonial, required a formal treatment of the paths and roads, and that a certain grove of fine old shade trees had to be cut down to secure a desired view. What could I say? The damage was done. I did not want to make my friend unhappy by insisting on his mistakes. Moreover, it would probably be lost effort, for it is just such serious mistakes, evident at once when attention is called to them, that the owner of the place will not see, because he thinks he cannot afford to see them. Just think of it! Here was a great river, a high bluff, and a fine oak-grove—one of those groves that would have delighted the souls of the old Greeks or Abraham the Patriarch. It was only necessary to shift the situation of the house a hundred feet, and rearrange the paths and roads, and the desirable views would have been retained, and the grove not only saved to support and protect the house from wind and storm, but made a genuine artistic background for the house itself. As it was the grove was mutilated to get a vista, and the house stood off on the bluff, lonely and unrelated to the grove or any other of the best features of the place. There was little or nothing of the systematic composition of a picture which should characterize the arrangement of all country places, both large and small.

I have referred to this country place of my friend to show the importance of selecting properly the site, not only that the architect may exhibit his house to advantage, but that the house may be duly coordinated with the distinctively interesting and artistically important features of the place. It should always be remembered, in undertaking to select the site even on the smallest places, that every plot or territory of ground has characteristics peculiar to itself, and to no other plot of ground; that it is undulating in a certain way; that it has agreeable or disagreeable outlooks; in a word, that it always has a distinct individuality of its own. The true way to manage it, therefore, from the standpoint of one who wishes to develop the entire beauty of his place, is to study all the features, good and bad, and tone down the bad ones and accentuate the good ones.

More mistakes are made in selecting sites than in almost anything else in landscape architecture. People think of only some one important consideration of the arrangement, and forget everything else. The house is not the only important feature of the place. It should not be allowed to obtrude itself, to be a discord in the picture, and obscure other important and charming features.

There are no definite rules, of course, that will always apply to the selection of a site for the house. Usually it should not be placed exactly in the middle of a place, or close to the front, and it should associate itself in some way with some considerable plantation of trees that may already exist.

I am speaking of considerations that must be met in a systematic way, and more or less in accordance with the best practice of the art of landscape gardening. But avoid being too conventionally artistic. Use common sense, and first of all make your grounds comfortable and convenient; then do what you can for the æsthetic. The latter may, in your opinion, be of the most importance, but the former, be sure, will, sooner or later, revenge itself on you for any undue neglect.

Remember, I am speaking now of all country places, meaning thereby a lot that may be only 25 feet by 100 feet, or may be five or six acres. In any case you are devising a picture when you undertake to lay out your grounds, even in the most simple fashion; and any arrangement that will develop and present with the best effect the most artistically valuable features, should be invariably chosen, though at first it may seem odd, and not in accordance with your conventional ideas of landscape gardening art. Any evident attempt at mere oddity is, of course, bad, and destructive of the harmony of the general arrangement; but there may be an unusualness of treatment that *seems* odd, though in reality effective and harmonious, simply because it is unconventional.

Take the carriage or foot entrances of a place as an illustration. Usually they are arranged at a little distance, twenty or thirty feet from the boundary lines of either side of the place, but frequently the most effective way to enter is exactly at the extreme corner of the lot, continuing across it. This is certainly not a conventional method, and yet it is an effective one.

Having selected the site of the house, and entered the place in such a way as to develop and perfect its essential beauties and attractions, let us see what we should next consider in the arrangement of our grounds.

Perhaps we can only have a foot-path on account of the small size of our place, and perhaps a carriage-drive may be admissible when we have grounds of two or three acres in extent. This path or drive should be laid out and constructed before the actual grading and planting is done. The arrangement of lawn and plants is as dependent on the situation and grades of the roads and paths as on the location of the house.

The first thing you must require of a road or path is that it shall reach the house by a sufficiently direct course to serve the general convenience of the place. Keeping this in view, a certain deviation may be allowed that will permit a better distant view, or the exhibition of some peculiar attraction of the lawn or plantations. As a rule, straight lines, absolutely straight lines, are to be avoided in landscape gardening. The slightest winding in a road or path almost invariably renders it more attractive. As with all rules, this one has its exceptions. It may be specially effective, under some peculiar circumstances, to arrange a straight avenue to the house, with a formal line of trees on either side ; or the architecture of the house may be such as to suggest on its immediate borders some form of the rectangular French or Italian style of gardening. Always avoid, if possible, sharp and sudden curves in your roads or paths, and also equal reverse curves—that is, curves that exactly repeat each other.

The width of roads and paths is another consideration that must necessarily depend on circumstances. Ordinarily, in a small country place, I have found a path of five feet and a road of thirteen feet ample, but it may be quite as reasonable in some cases to make the foot-paths eight feet and the carriage-drives fifteen feet. As to the question, How shall I construct my roads and paths ? much depends on the nature of the soil and on how much the paths and roads are to be used. Ordinarily it is wise to lay a foundation of broken stone six inches deep under all paths and one foot under drives for the sake of drainage, covering them with fine gravel and a little clay.

Continuing the carriage-drive up to the front door, we are met by the question, Shall we make a circle or an oval for the convenience of turning? Again, no one can say that an oval or a circle might not be suitable under certain circumstances. Ordinarily, however, we should avoid these forms, particularly the circle. There will be, usually, a tree or rock, or you can plant or place one, that will determine more or less the form of the turn. The shape is not of so much importance so long as it conforms to lines that will enable a carriage to turn with ease and without a tendency to run over the borders. I have found that such a turn should be at least forty feet across in its widest part, with its curves carefully adjusted to the easy turning of an ordinary carriage.

Subsidiary roads for bringing supplies to the house should be, of course, minimized and kept out of sight as much as possible; but if convenience requires them, no mere æsthetic considerations should prevent their employment. Paths should be likewise allowed only as a comparatively straight and easy way to reach a house or view.

All roads and paths are, indeed, only admissible as means of reaching a structure or view; otherwise the place would always look better without them. They have no attractions comparable with that of grass, flowers, shrubs, and trees. This should be remembered whenever the question of making a path arises. On consideration, perhaps, you will find that you will have to sacrifice more than you will gain, and the path will stay unmade. On the same principle, try to minimize the area of the open, bare spaces necessarily made by the meeting and crossing of paths and roads.*

After the paths and roads are made, there comes the preparation and grading of the lawns. Manure heavily and plow or dig deeply, and the superior growth of your grass will abundantly repay you. If you want a perfect piece of greensward, even and free from weeds, let me commend to you the use of carefully selected sods. There is no other way of making such perfect grass; but then, I must acknowledge, the lawn should be small or the expense of sodding must be

---

* See Landscape Gardening, by the same author.

necessarily great. In any case, the borders of the drives and walks, made level for a foot or two at least, whatever the steepness beyond, should be sodded. You will hardly make grass-seed produce a good permanent border in a year or two along the immediate edge of a path or road. It will be trodden too much, or suffer greatly from other vicissitudes incident to such places.

A word also should be said about the parallelism of the two sides of roads or paths. Ordinarily, as everyone knows, the width of a walk or road is kept the same throughout its extent. This is common-sense that is also conventional, but that does not preclude the wisdom of a systematic variation of the width of paths and roads wherever convenience requires. Perhaps a tree may force a widening, because the preservation of the tree is of more importance than the adherence to the conventional rule of parallelism of path- and road-lines. Sometimes, moreover, the necessity for a seat, or at least the space for the lingering of several pedestrians, will suggest a widening. I do not say that one should seek to be odd and different in his methods by frequently widening the paths, but simply that he should not be slavishly bound by a fancied necessity for adhering to the parallelism of road- and path-lines.

In grading the lawn we should be largely governed by the original topography of the ground, by its special idiosyncrasy, of formation, if I may be allowed the use of such a term in this connection. If the lawn be hollowing, don't attempt to fill it up, if you are not troubled by difficulties of drainage; and even then a land basin and a pipe led a short distance will often obviate this difficulty entirely. Sometimes even you will find it best, in the interest of developing the peculiar character of the place, to deepen the hollow of the lawn. Then again, part of the lawn may be hollow and part convex, and yet you must not attempt to make it level. To say that a level lawn is not, under most circumstances, desirable, seems to be a paradox. But it is a fact based on sound principles of art. Moreover, in most cases, you will hardly be able to make a level, absolutely level, lawn, hard as ever you may try. Of course, you should smooth off the asperities of the surface and secure easy-flowing lawn contours. Sometimes you can improve the effect of the undulations by judiciously arranged planting. But never, or only in the rarest cases, plant the crown of the convex portions of your lawn and bottom of your hollows. You will only thereby lessen the attractive variety and picturesqueness of the surface. Every contour, every line of a well-arranged place, will be always changing to the eye, not abruptly and suddenly, but harmoniously and gracefully. There must be no monotony of line anywhere —in walks, roads, grass surface, or plantations.

Concerning the plantations I should have much to say did space permit, for on them depends largely the successful composition and coloring of the place. The first thing to consider before you begin to plant is the adjustment of your views, vistas, or outlooks. Ordinarily, except where you require for some reason a special outlook, the entire outside border of the place should be planted with a mass of trees and shrubs, making a hedge of irregular, waving lines. Ordinarily, too, there should be something like seven shrubs to every tree, the shrubs standing eight or ten feet apart and the trees forty to fifty feet. This rule applies, of course, to only large-growing shrubs; the smaller ones can be tucked in round about. It is an excellent plan to establish a lofty tree, like the elm, tulip, or poplar, at each marked angle of the place and at either side of the carriage entrance. It tends to give character to the entire lawn. If you have room enough, one of the ways of emphasizing certain interesting parts of your country place, and especially the pleasant home character of the house, is to establish a grove near that building. Set out the best shade-trees—elms, maples, beeches, tulip-trees, liquid ambars, and lindens—and let them stand forty or fifty feet apart, so that they may grow into broad and lofty trees, dispensing abundant shade. Such a grove near the house will give perpetual delight throughout the year. Even in winter, during snow- and ice-storms, you will find unfailing pleasure in contemplating the unexpected and magical effects of snow and ice in your grove, and moreover find comfort in seeking its protecting shelter if you have planted a few pines in the midst. Planting groves means to many people simply the setting out of a cluster of trees eight or ten feet apart and allowing them to slowly crowd each other to death. Properly managed, the grove may be the most delightful and admirable feature of all country places, except the smallest, and even there one great elm or beech may be a grove in itself.

In adjusting the vistas by means of your planting, you should see that the longest lines of view are secured. Let them extend diagonally from corner to corner of your place if you can. It will give breadth and largeness to the treatment of the entire territory that will greatly enhance its attractiveness. Try also to mass your lawn into as large and open unplanted spaces as possible. It increases the much-to-be-desired breadth of the place.

At all intersections of paths, at entrance-gates, etc., there should be planted intermingled masses of trees and shrubs, so arranged that the way for the paths and roads may seem to have been hewn through them. I have named some good trees, among which should have been included the white birch and yellow wood or cladastris tinctoria. Let me also give you the names of some thoroughly excellent shrubs, not merely rare kinds, but such as you can readily find in most well-stocked nurseries. Here they are : Spiræa opulifolia, California privet, Japanese snowball, common snowball, standard honeysuckles, weigelas, Philadelphuses, Japan quince, purple berberry, Thunberg's spiræa, lilacs, hydrangea paniculata grandiflora, white fringe, purple fringe, and golden elder.

Don't plant trees and large shrubs close to the house. It gives a crowded feeling and is apt to obstruct the view from the windows. Small-growing shrubs may, however, be used effectively adjoining the house. They are not only beautiful in themselves, but they tend to mask the base of the house, where there is usually a sharp and uninteresting angle. A few specimens of shrubs and trees may be allowed to adorn the turn in front of the house, and those only immediately on the edge of the curves, so as to leave the green sward of the general surface of the turn open and free. If possible, make the surface also slightly undulating here as elsewhere.

Against one thing let me warn the reader, and that is the indiscriminate use of formal foliage or flower-beds on most lawns. They are apt to lend a garish and vulgar air to the place. Close to the house you may sometimes use one or two of these beds, but their bright red and yellow colors should be set a little on one side and not allowed to glare at one too much. I respect the universal delight in rich color, but all formal patches of color should be used carefully and in proper relations to the whole picture. A discordant mass of color hurts the eye much in the same way as a voice or instrument annoys the ear when not used in harmony. It is far more harmonious and satisfactory in most cases to employ, instead of beds of geraniums and coleuses, the hardy herbaceous plants, such as phloxes, lilies of the valley, harebells, larkspurs, hollyhocks, blue gentians, and the like, tucked away in the edges of groups of trees and shrubs.

I think I have now given a few important suggestions concerning some of the principles of treatment that apply alike to both small and large country places. But in order to illustrate better what I mean, I propose to ask the reader's attention for a brief space to an account of the treatment of a small place of five or six acres situated on the banks of the East River, ten or fifteen miles from New York [p. 146]. This place had a somewhat curious history. Thirty-five or forty years ago one of the wealthy men of New York bought it, probably because he was attracted by its bold position on a point or bend of the shore of the river. On this tract of land he planted at the time a considerable assortment of shade-trees and a few shrubs. There were elms, maples, beeches, poplars, lindens, pines, spruces, and other trees of similar character.

In the course of time these trees grew to great dimensions, for the soil was naturally rich and mellow, and excellently adapted to the growth of trees. The place remained in the hands of the family of the purchaser, who has been long dead, for the term of a generation, until the tract became a great thicket of saplings interspersed with full-grown specimens. Here and there along the river bank was a grove of pine and other trees standing free, but in main part the tract was a close-set wilderness.

Country Place of Six Acres on the East River, near New York.

A purchaser for the place finally came, eight or ten years ago, and undertook to make a home for himself. The tract, of course, looked like a tangle, although there were evidently fine trees scattered about. Many people would have started in with an axe and soon swept most of the wilderness away. But the present owner recognized capabilities and idiosyncrasies pertaining to the place that he thought charming, and therefore he proposed to develop them. The place was to be made a genuine woodland home a few miles from New York City. Let us see how he accomplished his purpose.

In the first place, at the southwest corner there stood an enormous elm-tree, just a few feet within the boundary line. This he conceived the idea of making the key-point of his entrance from the corner, thus turning the course of the drive diagonally across his land. Eventually the art displayed in carrying this winding road, with the lines of a gently flowing river, almost directly to the house, constituted one of the principal charms of the place.

At first the road went into the thicket with a sharp curve around the elm, and then straight away until it almost reached the house, when it turned suddenly around a "circle" or carriage sweep. By this means you saw nothing of the place and house until you had gone many yards beyond the entrance, and even then you only caught glimpses of the house till you came right upon it, whereas it was in reality all the time only a short distance away. Yet you did not feel shut in, because just after you left the elm-tree and passed the entrance of the winding foot-path that commenced here to skirt the place, a tennis-ground of an acre in extent spread out before you. This gave a charming effect of openness and let in at its farthest boundary the western sun and a noble view of the river. This was literally all the clearing that had been made, except in front of the house, where enough trees had been chopped out to prepare a small carriage turn about a grass plot forty feet in its largest diameter. The house was a low two-story structure, utterly unpretentious, but comfortable and convenient. Near the front gate a road wound off to the outbuildings and vegetable gardens in such a way that you would hardly discover it unless you were keeping a sharp look-out. A foot-path meandered by an almost secret way from the house to the barn. An acre and a half would probably comprise all the land that had been cleared from the original seven or eight acres, and really you would hardly realize, except just about the house, that any trees had been removed, so deftly had the work been managed in order to retain the original spirit and chief beauties of the place.

Don't understand that there was not a great deal of work laid out, because there was; but it was of a dainty, unobtrusive kind that simply developed and perfected existing charms. There was, for instance, not a formal flower or foliage bed on the place, but all along the borders of the woodland, skirting the tennis-ground, and in nooks everywhere along the walks that skirted the entire grounds, there were quantities of hardy herbaceous plants—harebells, irises, blue gentians, crocuses, phloxes, daffodils, in fact, wild flowers of many kinds, besides those found growing naturally on the place. Shrubs, especially American shrubs, were planted along the same borders wherever weak spots in the foliage occurred. The only planting which was evidently made for ornament came close to the house, where, with a background of woods, grew irregular groups of rhododendrons and azaleas, with two or three choice and beautiful specimens of evergreens of low growth.

The walk skirting the place was a mere narrow foot-path two or three feet wide, that sought all the most beautiful spots on the banks of the river which bounded the tract on two sides. At the points where the views were finest the path was widened for rustic seats, from which one might gaze at ease on the near and distant stretches of shining river. The rest and repose and perfect woodland charm of the spot, looking out on the river laden with numerous busy craft, was possessed of a unique charm that I have not words to express. There was a pine-grove also that I specially affected. It was open and airy, with the branches far up and a clean carpet of brown needles beneath, and as the wind played the peculiar tune of the pines and the glimpses of the river flashed near by, I often thought that here was a grove before which one might well lift one's hat in admiration.

There was nothing careless or unkempt about the place. It was tidy, the plants were thriving, the grass was vigorous and well kept, and the branches of the great trees were duly pruned; and yet it was all so unobtrusively natural that the wood-robins and other birds seemed to make it their home instinctively.

A Country Place of Seven Acres, with Pond, in the Midst of Open Country.

But the estate I have described was originally wooded and level, and situated on the banks of a great busy river. Let us consider for a few moments a place in Madison, N. J., where the original conditions were different. It will serve to suggest, and perhaps solve, for the reader several other problems that are likely to confront him [p. 149].

The peculiarity of this lawn was that the house stood on a high knoll that sloped down steeply to a lake of an acre and a half in extent. A stone bridge crossed a narrow stream a few yards in length, which connected this pool of water with a larger one above. In order properly to solve the problem of treating a high hill with the house on the apex and a pond below, the carriage-road was carried around a pear-shaped turn in front of the house. This turn was about forty feet in its largest diameter. Branch roads started out from this main road for the convenience of reaching the back of the house and the barn and stables. The points where these branches tapped the main road were, of course, heavily planted with shrubs and trees, so as to partially conceal the presence of the minor drives and the existence of the outbuildings. The main drive wound in one long curve around the easiest contour lines of the hill, thus securing comparatively good grades for a road traversing a steep hilly territory.

At every abrupt turn of the road masses of trees and shrubs were thrown across both sides, in order to mask the exact nature of the changes, and please by their variety and unsuspected nature. On reaching the bank of the lake the road was carried along at a sufficient distance from the water, ten or fifteen feet, to enable water-loving trees and shrubs to grow, such as willows, poplars, alders, etc. After winding along the bank four hundred or five hundred feet, the road finally came out on the main highway through a heavy stone gate covered with Japan ivy (Ampelopsis tricuspidata) and masked with groups of trees and shrubs. The road, which, after crossing the stone bridge, ran northeast along the base of the house-lot hill, was bordered inside the fence by an irregular plantation or hedge of trees and shrubs; and up around the house were scattered large shade-trees, such as elms, maples, beeches, and lindens.

The shores of the lake were further decorated here and there on prominent parts with water-loving trees and shrubs, and, above all, the edges of the lake were carefully sodded, so that the greensward dipped everywhere into the water. Standing on the road a little this side of the bridge, and looking on the still surface of the lake, one could see the whole green hill-side with the house and trees charmingly mirrored. Both ends of the stone bridge, I should have said, were masked with trees and shrubs and vines.

The place just considered was about seven acres in extent and on a hill. I will now ask the reader to consider a place of similar size, situated in the same region of New Jersey, which consisted of a deep hollow instead of a hill, and had no water or water views. The whole interior of this place was charmingly varied with natural groves of oak interspersed with a few pines [p. 153].

The general character of the main part of the interior had been left untouched, except that some of the trees in the lowest part had been cut out to reveal the full depth of the little valley. This was intended to carry out the general principle I have endeavored to impress on the reader already in this paper, that he should seek as much as possible to increase the variety of the surface, that is, make, if anything, the hills higher and the valleys deeper. At certain points of the heavily bordering woodland two or three fine views were opened to the blue hills in the extreme distance.

The entrance to this place was arranged in a somewhat peculiar fashion. It came on the extreme outside edge of the valley or bowl at a point nearest the highway. A hundred feet or so within the grounds the drive reached the house, which stood on a small level platform of made earth extending out to a sharp declivity, and just allowing enough space for the house and drive and a turn around beyond it. The view from the front door was charming, and a walk winding along the exterior lines of the place revealed many beautiful spots. No planting in this case was used, except about the gateway and on and about the turn in front of the house. The existing attractions of valley and native plantations were greater than any that could be added, and additions would probably be somehow out of harmony with the natural-

A Place of about Seven Acres in a New Jersey Hill Town.

ness of the scene. To this end pruning, fertilizing, and the sowing of grass-seed were practised yearly.

Of a similar hilly character was a place I once helped to arrange in Lenox, Mass. Its peculiarities were its smallness of size and nearness to an important highway, where all the fashion passed by. It was only an acre in extent, but was elaborately constructed of rocks, terraces, and the most rare and choice specimen trees and shrubs that could be obtained. The land originally sloped sharply down from the street, so that the house perforce was raised upon high walls and terraces on three sides. In front the land, however, was filled up so as to be comparatively level, sloping only moderately up to the street. There were rare and beautiful evergreens, such as the varieties of silver firs, pines, retinosporas, spruces, rhododendrons, hardy azaleas, Japanese maples, etc. For the sake of variety the carriage-road wound, with one or two comparatively sharp curves, a hundred feet or so along the front of the house, and so around a carriage turn made by a widening of the road, and out at the other gate. The stable stood near this gate, but was well masked with large trees and shrubs. Behind the house, on the level spaces made by the terraces, was arranged a flower-garden consisting chiefly of herbaceous and annual flowering plants, set out specially for the purpose of securing plenty of flowers for gathering. This place, by means of the variety of the curves of its roads, the number of its interesting features of trees, shrubs, flowers, and greensward, and, in a word, by its possession of a great share of landscape beauty in a comparatively small space, was and remains a model of its kind.

There was another country place of moderate dimensions that I call to mind, that possessed certain peculiar features worthy of consideration. It was situated near both the Harlem and the Hudson Rivers, and commanded fine distant views, and had the same high, hilly character as the place in New Jersey. [See Frontispiece.] This place, however, though seven acres in extent, had no lake, and had a large formal vegetable garden and distant barns and stables. There were many large and fine evergreens on the place, and the main road has been led to the east door, where a turn is provided. It then passes on by the house and a short distance down toward the barn, where another turn is secured on comparatively level ground. The space allowed by the steep slope directly in front on the other side of the house, and once used for a contracted turn, has been therefore thus abandoned. Broad lawns have been kept open, and distant views preserved in arranging the plantations; and a large croquet-ground has been laid out, with a summer-house beyond. The barns have been all shut out with masses of foliage, and the boundary lines with irregular hedges of trees and shrubs. One peculiarity of this place was its groups made up of some single kind of shrub; that is, you will find here a great group of weigelas, there one of spiræas, and yonder one of snowballs. I do not say that any one of these groups was made up of only one kind of shrub, but that a large majority were of one kind. Merely dotting about on the lawn a great variety of trees and shrubs, one or two of a kind, is rarely good lawn planting. You should have enough of a kind grouped together to properly exhibit its special mass effect.

I once laid out a place in Kentucky that, I think, illustrated well what could be done on an acre or two that was comparatively level, and inclined to be slightly monotonous in general effect. It was in a town, on a public street, and its width was one hundred and fifty feet and its depth four hundred and fifty. Apparently there was not much variety to be secured; yet much was really attained. In the first place, the entrance was arranged in the extreme corner of one side of the place. Notice how this arrangement gave a comparatively wide lawn on your right hand as you entered the place. Trees and shrubs, of course, shut out your view just at the gate, but in a moment a half-acre lawn opened out with a tree or two and a background of shrubbery. A smaller lawn lay across the road to the left hand, and then about a hundred feet from the entrance the road divided right and left into two branches, which, after hugging the exterior boundaries of the place, enclosed an ample central lawn of another half acre.

On reaching the house, two hundred and fifty feet from the gate, the two winding roads united again, and passed in a straight line one side of the house to the stables, leaving on the way, in front of the kitchen door, an ample widening for the carts of butcher and baker. Heavy plantations screened this road and its widening and allowed another open half-acre lawn, ornamented with choice single specimen trees, and backed by a portion of the same irregular hedge that surrounded the whole. There were magnolias, weeping beeches, weeping elms, red flowering horse-chestnuts, and Kentucky coffee-trees.

In front of the house across the road was a great wide-spreading American elm, and a little further on, bordering the drive, a rich-colored plant bed of coleus, geranium, and alternautheras. All along the

Grounds of a House at a Summer Watering Place.

drives, on either side, and about forty to fifty feet apart and ten feet back, grew fine shade-trees—the American linden, the tulip-tree, the purple beech, the liquid ambar, the Norway maple, and the white birch. Entirely around the place were planted irregular hedges of trees and shrubs, with here and there openings for looking out at some agreeable view.

Of yet simpler nature and more unpretentious character was a place I knew at Narraganset Pier, R. I. [p. 156]. To remember that it was on the seashore, and was level, with sandy soil, is to bring its limitations within a small compass. The house had been originally arranged, more by accident than design, in the middle of the plot. In order, therefore, to secure comparatively wide and long open side lawns the two entrances were brought nearer together than usual, directly in front of the house, and only twenty-five feet apart. The drives then led, in a long, narrow horseshoe-shaped curve, a hundred feet to the front door. A back entrance was arranged at the extreme rear of the lot within ten feet of its limit, and by a straight road the butcher and the baker were led to an ample turn before the kitchen door. This road was well masked with shrubbery standing two or three irregular rows deep. The remainder of the planting, however, was limited to a single waving border of shrubs, with occasional shade-trees, extending around the exterior boundary of the place. A half dozen low shrubs were used near the house, such as the Japan rose, Rosa rugosa, Philadelphus aureus nanus, etc. By this arrangement comparatively large lawns were secured and the greatest breadth of treatment possible under the circumstances.

The grass was not very strong, but was kept green and fresh-looking by fertilizing and watering. The shrubs and trees, on account of their exposed seashore position, were the toughest and hardiest kinds, such as laurel-leaved willow, American elm, balsam poplar, honey locust, California privet, standard honeysuckle, spiræa opulifolia, viburnum plicatum and V. dentatum, philadelphuses, weigelas, altheas, and hydrangea paniculata grandiflora.

The last place the treatment of which I am going to consider, though not strictly within my title, is a large city lot in Baltimore, Md. In size this lot was about one hundred and fifty feet deep and seventy-five feet in width or frontage on the street. Back from the street sixty feet stood the house, or houses, for the use of two brothers, with an open court-yard between. These houses were elegant and expensive. The rear yard was, of course, small, but really deep enough for all practical purposes [illustration below].

And now let me explain the peculiarity of the treatment of the front-door yard of these two houses that made it much more attractive than most places of the kind. You will notice that if the yard, seventy-five feet wide, had been divided into two of thirty-seven and a

Rural Treatment of a Place of Two Lots in a City.

half feet each, both would have been insignificant in size, but see the way the one common lawn was treated so as to give it the greatest possible apparent breadth and variety of effect. At three irregular points, about twenty feet apart, entrances for foot-paths were made, thereby disguising any sign of a dividing line between the two places, and giving each one a separate walk of his own. In the centre a path common to both families was allowed to wind (for all these paths wind). The outside paths clung close to the outer boundary, thus securing the greatest space possible for open lawns. At three corners or nooks of these paths rustic summer-houses were contrived, and from these and other points vistas were carefully managed. On the outer boundaries of the lot and sparsely along the paths were disposed the finest specimens of the rarest trees and shrubs that could be obtained. There were rhododendrons, azaleas, Japanese maples, dwarf magnolias, kalmias, Thunberg's berberry, in fact all kinds of plants that were not only rare and beautiful, but especially such as possessed a symmetry and elegance of their own befitting the dignity and finished art of a city door-yard or lawn. The turf being, after all, the most important feature of a city place, was also kept in the most exquisite order by incessant weeding and watering and by yearly fertilizing.

BUILDING AND LOAN ASSOCIATIONS

By W. A. LINN

WHEN men of small means found out that a business enterprise which no one of them could conduct alone was possible for them by uniting their labor and their capital, they discovered the secret of co-operation.

When they found out that by uniting their surplus earnings they could provide themselves with homes of their own, instead of remaining subject to the demands of landlords, they put co-operation to one of its most beneficent uses.

This kind of co-operation is most popularly known under the name of Building and Loan Associations; but the official title differs in different places. In England the common designation is "Building Societies." Those formed under the New York statute of 1887 must be called "Co-operative Savings and Loan Associations." In Massachusetts they were first styled "Co-operative Saving Fund and Loan Associations," a title which was changed by a later act to "Co-operative Banks." But, whatever their title, the object and general plan of operation are the same.

Exactly how long ago this kind of co-operation was devised is uncertain. But if we discard as unverified the statement that the essential principle of our modern Building and Loan Association system was known and employed during the Greek republic and among the Anglo-Saxons in England, we can still find for it a verified origin ancient enough to prove that it is no novel scheme of a speculative age.

H. F. A. Davis, a very intelligent writer on the subject, gives Birmingham, England, as the place, and the year 1781 as the date, of the first known association formed for the object of assisting its members to build or purchase houses. In the earliest association described, each member paid in 10s. 6d., on each share of stock he held, every month. A subscriber for three shares was entitled to have "one or more houses built for him of the value of 200 guineas;" a subscriber for two shares, one or more houses of the value of £140; and a subscriber for one share, "a single house, value £70." By 1795 "Building Clubs" had become common in Birmingham. The rules or by-laws of the "Greenwich Union Building Society" have come down to us from those early days; and it is curious to note how closely they resemble the by-laws of the best-planned associations in this country to-day. A notable difference is, however, that the membership was limited to fifty. The legality of such organizations under the common law seems first to have been called in question in some proceedings in which this last-named society was a party. And, the suit having terminated in its favor, we are told that "similar societies were formed in other parts of the country, Scotland, Lancashire, and South Wales being the districts where they were most popular." The Earl of Selkirk, a philanthropic man of wealth, was instrumental in establishing a society at Kirkcudbright, Scotland, in 1815. The system must have proved a steady success, for the number of societies or associations has kept on increasing throughout Great Britain, reaching 2,050 by the year 1851, with an annual income of £4,000,000; and returns made to Parliament showed that, in July, 1888, the societies numbered 2,404, with assets of £54,200,620 and a membership of over six hundred thousand.

Edmund Wrigley, a leading American writer on the subject, fixes the date of the introduction of the Building and Loan Association system in this country at about the year 1840. Philadelphia seems to have seized most readily on the idea; but associations were also formed not only in other Northern cities, but in Charleston, Savannah, and other cities in the South and West. At first they were organized without the assistance of special statutes regarding them; their managers, for instance, being trustees appointed by deed. But as experience gave wisdom, the aid of the Legislatures was sought; and now in almost, if not quite, every State where interest in the matter has been excited, there are laws governing the organization and management of such corporations. As this legislation generally has not yet reached a state of perfection which requires exact statistical returns, as in the case of bank legislation, the number of these organizations in this country, their membership, and their assets, cannot be given precisely.

A conservative calculation, however, places the number of associations doing business in this country at between 5,000 and 6,000, with a probability that it may exceed the latter figures. Pennsylvania leads the list with 1,200, Ohio is second with 800, and Illinois and Indiana come next with 600 and 400, respectively. New England is credited with 175, the Southern and Southwestern States with 825, Nebraska and Iowa with 200, and California with 100. In the way of exact statistics, the Banking Department of New York for 1892 reports 415 associations in that State, with a total membership of 134,574, outstanding shares numbering 1,308,921, and assets of $28,049,736. The report of the New Jersey Labor Bureau for the same year shows that there are 272 associations in that State, having 78,700 members, owning 518,000 shares, and with assets of $25,600,000. Judge Seymour Dexter estimates the assets of all the associations in the United States at $455,454,000, the membership at 1,410,000, and the annual receipts at $180,000,000.

There has been some discussion about the effect of the rapid growth of the building and loan association system on savings bank deposits. Mr. F. B. Sanborn, in a report to the Social Science Association in 1888, estimating the investment in the Minnesota associations at $18,000,000, said: "The deposits in Minnesota savings banks hardly exceed $2,000,000; and the rapid growth of these associations has certainly checked the growth of savings banks there as it has in Rochester and Buffalo, N. Y., in Pittsburg, and in every State west of the Alleghanies." A decrease of $893,703 in the deposits of the New York City savings banks in 1888, as compared with 1887, and of $346,-322 in those of Brooklyn, was attributed to the recent increase in the number of associations in those cities. On the other hand, the Labor Bureau report of New Jersey for 1892 says that the association movement there has "apparently not affected that of the savings banks," and it cites official figures showing that the New Jersey savings banks, which in 1869 had deposits of $11,551,369, had in 1892 deposits of $33,807,634. There is plenty of room for both of these agencies of thrift. But the truth doubtless is that different localities are affected differently by the competition. In the South the building and loan system is making rapid progress, while the savings bank has gained but a slender foothold there. As the accumulations under the building and loan system have amounted, in this country, in the last forty-five years, to something like $1,000,000,000, it is safe to assume that a part of this has been diverted from the savings banks.

What, now, is this system of co-operation which has stood so long a trial, has won its way so steadily and generally into popular favor, and has produced so wonderful financial results? Why does it commend itself to so many persons of small incomes, and why have failures under it been so rare?

A Building and Loan Association is a corporation, regularly formed in accordance with the law of its locality; generally, as I have explained, a statute especially adapted to this form of business. Its officers consist of a president, vice-president, secretary, treasurer, board of directors, and a counsel. There may be slight variations from this list. For instance, in some associations auditors and appraisers are included in the number of officers annually elected; while in others the auditors are chosen just previous to the close of the official year, to examine the secretary's accounts, and appraisers are appointed from time to time as loans are made. In small towns the secretary is the only salaried officer; in other places a salary is paid both to him and to the treasurer, and in some large associations in New York City and in the West the president receives compensation. Aside from the salaries, the expenses consist of the rent of a room for holding the meetings and receiving the dues, the cost of the necessary printing, and incidentals. Small associations pay rent for a room only one or two evenings in a week. Larger ones require more permanent accommodations. I can cite an association in a suburb of New York City which, in the first two years of its existence, issued 1,869 shares of stock and accumulated assets of $33,061, and whose total expenses for those years were about five hundred dollars. In cities like Philadelphia, where associations are very numerous, and the accounts of many series have to be kept in each, it is customary for one person to be employed as secretary by several, his duties becoming those of a professional accountant. To show the responsibility of such a position, an instance may be mentioned in which the secretary of six associations handled $4,939,728 from 1879 to 1886, inclusive.

The persons composing a Building and Loan Association agree to pay into their treasury a certain sum, at fixed periods, on each share that they own, until their shares through such payments and the accumulated profits reach their par value, or, as it is technically termed, "mature." The stated payments (called "dues"), their frequency, and the par value of the stock vary. The most general rule is that $1 shall be paid on every share once a month until a par of $200 is reached. When the shares "mature" the assets in the treasury are divided among the shareholders. Just as fast as the money is paid in it is offered in the shape of loans to the members—and to the members only—the security taken being a mortgage on real estate and an assignment to the association of the borrower's stock. The amount which a member is entitled to borrow equals the par value of his or her shares. Thus, in an association where the par value is $200, a member who wants $1,000 must own five shares. As every member has an equal right to become a borrower, the disposition of the loans is made by putting the money up at auction, from time to time, and awarding the loan to that member who will give the highest premium above the regular interest rate. The Building and Loan Association laws provide that the acceptance of these premiums shall not constitute usury. In order that the dues and interest shall be paid regularly, the by-laws provide that they shall be received only by the secretary, and by him only at the stated meetings; and there is a small fine for a non-payment, which is increased from meeting to meeting, a delinquency for a certain period causing the forfeiture of the stock, or giving ground for the foreclosure of a mortgage.

The interest is paid weekly or monthly, and the interest money, with the dues and any other receipts, goes into the treasury, to be loaned at once. It is apparent, therefore, that a Building and Loan Association whose money is in demand not only receives interest constantly on the dues paid in by all the members, but that *it compounds this interest*. Herein lies the chief secret of the profitableness of this system of investment.

To explain more particularly the operations of one of these associations (the details of management, of course, differ): The regular meeting night finds the secretary seated at his desk, with one or two of the directors at his side as tellers. The members, who are provided with pass-books, as in the case of savings bank depositors, hand in their dues (and interest, if borrowers) to the secretary, who enters the amount, receipts for it with his initials, and announces the name and deposit to the tellers, each of whom enters the same in a separate blotter. At the close of the evening each of these blotters must balance with the amount of money in the secretary's hands; if there is any error it is looked for at once. Thus a perfect check is placed upon the secretary. When the money is counted, the secretary pays it over immediately to the treasurer, who is required by the by-laws to deposit it in a designated bank within twenty-four hours. As the treasurer is under bonds, the money is safe while it is in his hands. For greater security it is customary, with some associations, to require the signatures of two directors to the association's checks, in addition to those of the president, secretary, and treasurer. During the course of the evening, when there is money on hand, some officer, usually the president, announces that a loan, or loans, will be made to the highest bidder or bidders. A member who thus becomes entitled to a loan, at once gives to the counsel a description of the property, with a plan of the house, if he intends to build a new one, and the premises are examined, as soon as practicable, by the association's appraisers. When the directors receive the appraisers' report they decide whether the loan is a safe one or not. In reaching this decision each application is considered on its own merits. A private lender would simply inquire if there was a good margin of value above the amount of the loan; but in the case of an association borrower the directors inquire into the applicant's personal character, and find out his employment and his salary, wages, or income. If this results satisfactorily, and the premises proposed to be bought are not beyond the applicant's means, then the directors can take into further consideration the facts that the borrower will begin to pay off his debt at the very next meeting of the association, and that experience has proved that a person who is securing a home in this easy way will make, in most cases, almost any sacrifice rather than see the property pass out of his hands. I have never seen a happier man than a German laborer who stood in front of a little house, just finished, which his Building and Loan Association had put up for him. And the pleasure expressed in his countenance seemed to me a better assurance that he would clear the debt from that house, than the bond of many a richer man would be that the latter would meet his payments. Dr. Keck, the pioneer organizer of these associations in Cincinnati, had to complain a few years ago that the desire for membership there was so great that "many people suffer by it—the butcher, the baker, the doctor, the tenant, the landlord." While this is an admission that the business may be overdone, it also shows how strong is the desire "to own a home" when once the way to do this is opened up to a man to whom it has seemed an impossibility.

Loans are made to members either to purchase houses already erected, to build houses, or to remove existing encumbrances. If a member borrows to build a new house, the money is not paid over to him in bulk, but is paid to the contractor, on the audit of the owner and the association's building committee, as the work proceeds.

One of the great advantages of these associations as assistants of persons of small means is, that they can safely lend very close to the appraised values. Seventy per cent. to a man of good habits is considered an excellent risk, and Mr. Paine, the Superintendent of the Banking Department of New York State, in a work recently published, says: "It is seldom that a loan of more than eighty per cent. of the appraised value of mortgaged property is absolutely secure."

The earliest Building and Loan Associations contemplated the issue of stock all of the same value, members joining at any time after the date of organization paying back-dues sufficient to effect this; and all the members were to continue the payment of their dues until maturity was reached, when the mortgages of the borrowers were to be cancelled, the non-borrowers would receive the par value of their shares in cash, and the life of the association would end. This was a perfectly feasible scheme, but there were reasons why it did not work with entire satisfaction. As an association grew older, the cash payment required of new members steadily increased, and the growth of membership ceased. In the course of time the list of would-be borrowers was exhausted, the funds remained inactive, and at best a large sum had to be accumulated to pay the shares of the non-borrowers. So the life of the association was prolonged beyond the original calculation.

To obviate this difficulty it has been found best to issue shares in successive "series," the present value of the shares of each series being kept equal, the funds of all being loaned together, and the profits being apportioned among the different series according to their age and assets. Such an association is called a "permanent" or "serial" one; the first-mentioned a "terminating" one. The frequency of the issue of new series is regulated by the demand—as quarterly, semi-annually, or annually. A "serial" association, too, presents this advantage: A member of an older series who has not borrowed on his shares may withdraw the amount to his credit when it equals the price of a lot, buy his land, enter a younger series, and in it borrow the money to erect his house. Thus a "serial" association is constantly creating for itself a body of borrowers, and borrowers, it must ever be kept in mind, are the life of the system.

The "terminating" plan still finds favor in some places, associations of this kind in Philadelphia being, it is said, for some unexplained reason, most popular among the Germans and Irish. In Reading, Pa., where there are a number, a reason given for not discarding the older plan is that members like to know that "an association *can* wind up and pay all its members," and that the fixing of a date for termination is a check on the concealment of mismanagement. To obviate the disadvantages above referred to, a new association, instead of a new series, is started every year, with practically the same officers, one secretary, for instance, acting for a dozen associations. But with honest management and intelligent book-keeping the serial plan is much less cumbersome.

In some States the total number of shares which an association may issue is limited by law. There are three statutes governing these corporations in New York. The older one (that of 1851) contains no limitation of this kind. By the statutes of 1887 and 1892 the outstanding shares of the value of $200 each cannot exceed 10,000. In Pennsylvania the limit is 2,500 shares of $200 each, and in Massachusetts 5,000 of the same value. In New Jersey, by an amendment passed in 1888, all limitation as to the number of shares to be issued by an association working under the serial plan is removed. Careful writers on the subject point out danger to an association whose shares become too numerous; but this danger, I would say, would be realized only in a large city where the number of associations did not increase, as usual, with the demands for stock. If 2,500 shares seem a small limit, it must be remembered that in a "serial" association there are constant transfers from one series to another, as well as voluntary withdrawals from membership and compulsory retirements.

A word of explanation about the latter. The essence of success in a Building and Loan Association is to keep all the funds in active operation—to have no money lying idle in the bank. But even in a "serial" association, if, as a series approaches maturity, any considerable number of non-borrowing shareholders remain, the officers will have to accumulate a cash fund to meet the matured value of their shares. The number of such investors is in practice found to be smaller than might be supposed, owing to the voluntary withdrawal of shares. But, to provide for an emergency, directors are—or should be—given authority to retire the shares of non-borrowing members from time to time, as their series grow older and the condition of the treasury warrants. The Massachusetts statute requires such withdrawals, and its text on this point may be cited as an illustration:

"The directors may, at their discretion, under rules made by them, retire the unpledged shares of any series at any time after four years from the date of their issue, by enforcing the withdrawal of the same; but whenever there shall remain in any series, at the expiration of five years after the date of its issue, an excess above one hundred unpledged shares, then it shall be the duty of the directors to retire annually twenty-five per centum of such excess existing at said expiration of five years after the date of its issue, so that not more than one hundred unpledged shares shall remain in such series at the expiration of nine years from the date of its issue; and thereafter the directors may in their discretion retire such other unpledged shares as they consider the best interests of the bank to require; provided, that whenever under the provisions of this section the withdrawal of shares is to be enforced, the shares to be retired shall be determined by lot, and the holders thereof shall be paid the full value of their shares, less all fines and a proportionate part of any unadjusted loss; provided also that shares pledged for share loans shall be treated as unpledged shares." In some associations the matured shares are allowed to continue as paid-up stock and to draw interest until it is convenient to pay them off.

To show how, in actual practice, the number of existing shares in older series decreases, I have compiled the following table of the existing number of shares, in six New Jersey associations, from the report of the State Bureau of Statistics of Labor and Industries for 1886:

NUMBER OF SHARES.

Oldest series	63	12	48	71	99	5
Next oldest	57	17	21	67	76	5
Next oldest	62	17	10	55	97	1
Next oldest	59	22	10	40	101	8
Next oldest	160	18	7	31	161	5
Next oldest	207	45	11	97	252	12
Next oldest	135	64	31	100	274	29
Next oldest	336	44	29	189	197	52
Next oldest	385	85	38	411	283	27
Next oldest	425	183	55	753	530	96
Next oldest	543	257	86	924	608	150
Next oldest	...	682	274	...	...	189

Members are allowed to withdraw their shares as they wish, so long as the total demand of this kind does not exceed a fixed limit at any one time; as, for instance, one-half of the dues of a month. This provides against a possible "run" on the association. Withdrawing members receive back their dues paid in, less fines and their share of any losses, and such proportion of accumulated profits as the by-laws of their association may provide. The earlier associations made no provision for the cancellation of mortgages before the maturity of the borrowers' shares, or none except where other members stood ready to borrow the money paid in. But experience showed that many persons were deterred from borrowing of an association without the privilege of removing the encumbrance at their convenience; as, for instance, if an opportunity occurred to make an advantageous sale of the property to some one who wanted to pay cash in full. It is coming to be the practice, therefore, to permit a borrower to pay off his mortgage at any time on a given notice, the money being either loaned again or used in retiring shares.

The most perplexing problem that presents itself to a person whose attention is first directed to the Building and Loan Association system of borrowing is this: How can a member be benefited by a loan on which he pays *a premium*, in addition to the regular rate of interest? It is well, therefore, that this feature of the system be perfectly understood.

At the start it must be remembered, first, that this premium is in reality only a payment made by a borrower for the privilege of having the immediate use of the par value of his shares, for which the non-borrower is obliged to wait a term of years; and, second, that the money in the treasury is put up at auction, in quest of a premium, only in order to give all the members an equal chance to secure it.* In England, and, I think, in this country, other plans of assigning loans have been tried. Sometimes they have been assigned by lot; but, under this scheme, the money would often go to members who did not care to use it, and they would dispose of it to other members at a premium which went into their own pockets. In other associations a list of applicants for loans has been made out, and the money paid over to them in turn; but this did not prove satisfactory.

Again, in considering the premium feature it must be remembered that, as the premiums all go into the common treasury, each payer

* Associations in which a minimum premium is fixed are, I think, very exceptional.

of a premium shares the premiums paid by all the other borrowers, and that the larger the average premiums, the greater are the profits of the association, and the sooner is the stock matured and the borrower's mortgage cancelled. I have heard the statement made, "I would rather belong as a borrower to an association whose money brings thirty per cent. premium than to one which gets only three or five, because my debt would be so much the sooner discharged." Practically, this only means that such a person is able to make larger payments in order to shorten the time. By the majority of members of such organizations easy payments are most desired.

Courts have held that the fixing of a minimum premium is illegal, but they have held that usury cannot be pleaded when the premium is determined by open competition. Thus the Supreme Court of New York (25 Barb., 263) so held, and the New York Court of Appeals (1 Abbott's Appeal Decisions, 347) has sustained this reasoning.

But let us look further into the profits of these associations, which premium-paying borrowers share.

If each member of a Building and Loan Association, the par value of whose stock is $200, contributed $1 a month to its treasury, and there were no expenses and no profits, the shares would mature in two hundred months, or sixteen years and eight months. But in a prosperous association, while the expenses are very small, every dollar that comes into the treasury is kept earning other dollars, the interest, as I have explained, being compounded monthly. The profitableness of this system of lending may be seen from the statement that while $1,000 at six per cent., simple interest, will earn only $300 in five years, it will, if the interest is compounded annually, earn 338.22\frac{6}{10}$, and, if the interest is compounded monthly, will earn 348.83\frac{2}{10}$; and the gain goes on increasing with every successive year. From this cause the members of a Building and Loan Association, instead of waiting sixteen years and eight months for their shares to become worth $200 each, find the par value attained in a much shorter period. And just as soon as this is attained a borrower's mortgage disappears.

Exactly how long a series of shares must run to reach maturity cannot be calculated precisely in advance, because it is impossible to foresee the rate of premiums offered, the expenses, the number of withdrawals, etc. An association—to use Wrigley's illustrations—that (1) makes a profit of ten per cent. per annum on the average time will mature its stock in ten years and ten months; (2) making thirteen and a quarter per cent., will mature in ten years; (3) making twenty-seven per cent., will mature in eight years. In calculating the withdrawal value of shares in associations using the "gross" or "net" system of paying premiums (to be explained hereafter), it is customary in this country to estimate the life of a series at ten years, and in England at twelve years. Albert Shaw, Ph.D., in his papers on "Co-operation in a Western City," published by the American Economic Association, says of the Mechanics' and Workingmen's Loan and Building Association of Minneapolis, which began business in 1874 with a membership of forty-five, and whose receipts are now from $80,000 to $90,000 a year: "The average premium bid for loans has been forty-two and one-eighth per cent., and the final cost to the borrower is about eight per cent., while the 'freeholders' (those whose shares remain unpledged to the close of the series) gain about twelve per cent. annual compound interest on their savings." These statements are sufficient to show that the premium need not be a cause of alarm to borrowers in these associations. At the same time I am an advocate of low premiums, and think the aim of the officers of an association should be to keep premiums down rather than to run them up.

But I may illustrate this fact very clearly by simple figures.

Suppose that A and B each borrows $3,000 at the same time, A of a Building and Loan Association on fifteen shares at five per cent. premium and six per cent. interest, and B of a private lender at the same rate of interest but without any premium, B to pay his principal at the same time that A's shares mature. Supposing that maturity is reached (1) in ten years and (2) in thirteen years, the two accounts will stand as follows:

1.	2.
A, Paid in monthly dues $1,800	A, Paid in monthly dues $2,340
Paid in interest 1,800	Paid in interest 2,340
Paid in premium 150	Paid in premium 150
Total payments $3,750	Total payments $4,830
B, Principal $3,000	B, Principal $3,000
Interest 1,800	Interest 2,340
Total payments $4,800	Total payments $5,340

Under the first example A pays $1,050 less than B, and under the second $510.

If the person of whom B borrows permits him to pay the interest and $180 (the amount of A's annual dues) of the principal annually, under the system of partial payments, it will require between thirteen and fourteen years to liquidate the debt.

A further analysis of these figures, that is sometimes made in Building and Loan Association prospectuses, is this: A's total payments in ten years being $3,750, and the principal actually borrowed on being $3,000, the total amount he has to charge to interest is $750 for the ten years, or $75 a year, which is at the rate of two and one-half per cent. per annum; or, if his series runs thirteen years, his interest charge is $1,830, or $140.77 a year, which is at the rate of four and seven-tenths per cent. per annum. Expert accountants, who have been employed to find flaws in the Building and Loan Association system, have made haste to point out that a member of an association continues to pay interest on the whole amount borrowed, while his dues are constantly decreasing that amount, and hence that this is only an apparent interest rate.* But the vital question with a person who borrows a few hundred or thousand dollars with which to secure a home, and which is to be paid back in small instalments, is, "How large a sum out of my income for the next ten or twelve years will be required to make my payments?" If anyone will lend him the required amount, with the understanding that he is to pay the principal at the end of ten or twelve years and only annual interest meanwhile, can he find any way in which to invest his accumulating principal (if he *does* accumulate it) which will so rapidly increase it to the required amount as the Building and Loan Association increases it for him? If he is A in the above examples, he will be a good way ahead of his neighbor B financially when their respective debts are paid. A's payments are small, systematic, and at the same time imperative. When he goes home from every meeting of the directors he says, "My house is so much nearer being my own." And when he attends a quarterly or annual meeting of his association at which the profits are reported, and he finds a sum to his credit beyond any that he has paid in, he learns, perhaps for the first time, the secret of making money saved earn other money.

It is quite as easy to show by figures the economy of buying one's house with the assistance of a Building and Loan Association as compared with paying rent. The following statement is only given as a form of comparison; every prospective borrower can change the figures to suit his own locality.

C and D occupy houses worth $3,000 each (lot, $600, and building, $2,400). C is a tenant, paying $25 per month. D, with $600 in cash, has borrowed $2,400 on twelve shares of a Building and Loan Association, and built his house. Supposing that D's shares

---

* In what has been called the "Ohio system" the dues paid in are deducted at stated periods from the principal, and interest is charged only on the remainder. As this necessarily prolongs the life of a series, the benefit to the borrower is more figurative than actual.

mature in twelve years, their accounts at the end of that period will stand thus :

> C has paid out $3,600 in rent, and has nothing to show for it.
> D has paid out: Monthly dues.......................$1,728
> Interest............................. 1,728
> Premium, five per cent. 120
> Search 50
> Taxes 260
> Insurance 100
> Interest on value of lot............. 432
> Total........................$4,418

The neighborhood must be a very inactive one where the increased value of the property will not more than offset the cost of repairs. We find, then, that D owns his premises by paying out only $818 more than C, who, at the end of the period named, has nothing to show for his money.

One or two things remain to be said in explanation of the premium system. There is constant discussion among writers on the subject about the advantages and disadvantages of very large premiums. As I have pointed out, *average* high premiums mean larger payments for a shorter time. An element of trouble comes in when high premiums in the early years of an association are followed by low ones later on. Then, evidently, the earlier borrowers pay a higher rate of interest than those who follow them. In actual practice, where no minimum premium is fixed, the amount bid will be regulated by the law of supply and demand. Start a pioneer association in a place of considerable size, where, for the first time, an opportunity is afforded to secure homes under this easy system of payments, and competition will probably run the premiums offered to a high figure ; and this rate may be kept up for a good many years in places like St. Paul and Minneapolis, whose growth is rapid and whose accession of wage-earners is constant. But with the demand for loans will certainly come new associations, an enlargement of the loan fund, and a diminution of premiums. Take, for example, the cities of New York and Philadelphia; the former has been very slow to take advantage of this kind of coöperation, most of its existing organizations being only a few years old. Premiums of sixty per cent., and perhaps more, have been paid for loans in New York within the last year. In Philadelphia, Mr. M. J. Brown, editor of *The Building Association and Home Journal*, writes me: "Very few associations are obtaining any premium on loans. Good borrowers can obtain all the money needed without a premium. The premium is no longer a factor here."

There are about thirty-five associations in New York City, and some four hundred and fifty in Philadelphia. Hence the difference. High premiums were once as eagerly offered in the latter place as they now are in the former.

There are different ways of paying the premium. Under what is known as the "gross plan" the premium is deducted in advance from the sum that is loaned, while interest is charged on the whole amount. Under the "net plan" the premium is deducted as before, but interest is charged only on the sum which the borrower receives. Under a third system, known as the "instalment plan," the premium is paid in monthly instalments. This last plan avoids many difficulties encountered under the others, as in calculating the value of shares at any time. A fourth method, sometimes practised, is to issue to a borrower additional stock whose par value shall equal the premium paid; this makes his payments of dues on the additional stock instalment payments. Still another plan which has been tried is to have the rate of interest determined by competition. This is again the instalment plan. A premium of five per cent. on the gross plan is equal to about eight cents per month on the instalment plan.

At first glance it might seem as if there was unfairness in the positions occupied in an association by the two classes of members, the borrowers and the non-borrowers, the former sharing the premiums and interest paid by the latter. But this is a superficial view. I doubt if any association is ever organized in these days in which those members who wish to borrow at one time supply the requisite sum in dues; so that immediate borrowers require the non-borrowers' assistance. Besides, a large class of borrowers is supplied from among those who may be mere investors at the start. As most associations lend only on first mortgage, requiring a borrower to own a fee in the land, many persons purchase shares who own no land and have no money to buy any, and very likely never would have any without the aid of some systematic plan of saving. But after they have been non-borrowing members for a certain time, they find that their savings are large enough to enable them to buy the coveted piece of land. So they withdraw their accumulations, secure their lots, take shares in a new series, and become borrowers in turn. The non-borrowers, too, are, or should be, liable to peremptory retirement whenever their assistance is no longer necessary.

Considered abstractly as a beneficial feature in a community, an association of this kind would be commendable if it only induced a number of persons to lay aside small sums every month, without paying them any profits. And it is the cultivation of the habit of saving which is one of the best arguments in favor of the Building and Loan Association system, especially as such associations can be formed where the establishment of a savings bank would be impracticable.

If complete statistics of these associations in this country and in Great Britain were available they would prove the safety of the system by showing the very small number of failures under it. But this plan of investment has not, in every case, worked satisfactorily, and it is well to consider the disappointments in order to warn investors and managers that it is possible to go astray.

I am informed that in the Western States and in Massachusetts, where so many associations have been for years in operation, no instance of a failure is on record. In the early history of the associations in Pennsylvania some of them did not work out satisfactorily; but this was because of ignorance in their Board of Directors. The premiums were paid on the "gross plan," and early retiring members were allowed so large a share of the apparent immediate profits that those who remained " came short," and the date of maturity was unduly prolonged. The largest list of failures and the fullest history of their causes are to be found in New York State.

Before the year 1851 several associations were organized in this city without the assistance of a legislative enactment. The popularity of the idea became so great that an "act for the incorporation of building, mutual loan, and accumulating fund associations" was passed by the Legislature in 1851, and it is stated that by 1856 one hundred and twenty-four of them were doing business in this State, while already it appears that more than thirty had gone out of existence. A reaction set in, and complaints by members were so frequent that the Legislature in 1855 appointed a special committee to investigate the subject and ascertain the cause of the trouble. Their report is numbered 46 in volume iii. of Assembly Documents. This report specifies two causes "which have had much to do with the creation and embarrassment of these associations." The one "was the commercial activity which followed the discoveries on the Pacific," and the other, "the commercial crisis consequent upon an extended trade which those discoveries had seemed to warrant." In the time of inflation almost everybody felt able to assume the responsibility of the payment of dues and interest, as well as a liberal premium. When hard times came members could not meet their payments, and when they found that their investments were likely to be lost through foreclosure, they appealed to the courts and the Legislature for relief. This cause of trouble might have affected only the defaulting members, and not the associations as a whole, but many of the early associations accepted second mortgages as security, and this, the report says, was one fruitful source of complaint. Mismanagement by the officers was also charged. The rush of withdrawals was so great that in some associations the receipts were put up at auction, and the person who would take the smallest sum for his shares was paid off first. The evils of the system seemed so great to this committee that they recommended a repeal of the act.

Judge Seymour Dexter, in a paper read before the Social Science Association in 1888, cited some failures outside of New York City. The first association organized in Rochester, in 1852, was wound up, having failed to realize the expectations of its members, probably from the causes just named. The next effort in that city was made nineteen years later, and in the ensuing years a number of associations were organized there; but some "Building Lot Associations," which had in view a real estate speculation, were also founded there at the same time. The latter came to grief, and having been confounded in the public understanding with Building and Loan Associations, these received much injury. Two or three associations in existence in Albany in 1871 lost heavily through bad management, some of their loans having been made on second mortgages. One association organized in Elmira, and another in Waverly, in 1871, were closed before maturity, with consent of the stockholders. An association started in Elmira, in 1875, began with by-laws accepting no premium of less than $40 a share (twenty per cent.). There was great demand for the stock at first, but when, after four or five years, the borrowing slackened, the minimum rate of premium was reduced one-half without obviating the trouble. Eight years ago the minimum premium was abolished entirely, and, we are told, "from that time the association began to grow in popularity. Its money was readily loaned, and, while it received only $62 on $40,750 borrowed in 1887, and $232 on $60,000 borrowed in 1868, it is maturing a series of shares every year to the satisfaction of its shareholders, ninety-five per cent. of whom are wage-earners." The age of each series is about eleven years. This Elmira example is worthy of study by anyone who thinks that large premiums are necessary to an association's prosperity.

Of the unsuccessful early New York associations, all, I believe, were organized on the "terminating and gross premium" plan.

The Legislature of Connecticut caused an investigation of the associations in that State to be made some thirty years ago, and in 1860 they were forbidden to receive deposits after January 1, 1862. In 1865 they were required to return their deposits to the shareholders by July 1, 1886. The system is, however, becoming popular again in that State.

The safety or the risk of this system of investment is increased directly in proportion as its original purpose is adhered to or departed from. As a means of speculation it should take no part. Well-managed associations limit the amount of stock which one member may hold, and, consequently, the amount of money which he can borrow. In some States this limit is fixed by law, as in Massachusetts, where the maximum is twenty-five shares; the New York act of 1875 limits the number of shares which a person may hold in one series to ten unpledged and twenty pledged.

Some localities are much better adapted to this form of co-operation than others. It would have a poor field in a Newport or a Lenox, where there is no considerable body of wage-earners. The more expensive land is in any place, the larger are the loans required by each member and the greater is the risk to the lender. The limited area of New York City makes it a less available field than Philadelphia, Chicago, and St. Paul, and largely, for this reason, it has been called a city of tenements, while the others boast that they are cities of homes. Where the membership is made up principally of persons who are not strictly wage-earners, the officers are likely to be men on whose time there are many demands, and who are not, therefore, regular in their attendance on the meetings. Complaints on this ground are made in regard to some New York City associations, and they are serious.

Attracted by the success of the strictly co-operative associations, corporations have been formed which profess to carry on the same business, and under the same name, but on a "national" plan, that is, to carry on a money-loaning scheme under the guise of a building and loan association, but to do so with the aid of expensive permanent offices, salaried officers, and paid solicitors, and to lend the money of the associations in all parts of the country. It is the latter feature of the business that has given them the name "national." I look on these concerns as dangerous to the really co-operative system, not because they are business rivals, but because they are masquerading under the name of the co-operatives on a system that is dangerous, and, consequently, because, when they come to grief, many people will confound their ruin with a radical weakness in the business methods of the co-operatives. When these "nationals" started out a few years ago (they are still creatures of tender years), they boasted loudly that they could offer inducements which no local association could equal, and they presented statements to indicate how low a rate of interest their borrowers would really pay when the stock matured, high as the rates of payment were. The expense account of the "nationals" was enough to prove the falsity of these promises. A local association pays a small salary to its secretary and its treasurer, and a small rent for the occasional use of a room. This covers almost all of its expense account. A "national," on the other hand, pays large rent for permanent offices, has a big salary list, aside from its agents' commissions, and incurs other expenses which a local knows nothing about.

The Superintendent of the Banking Department of New York, in his report for 1892, shows that while the percentage of expense of the local associations in that State for the year was about 2, that of the "nationals" was 11, and that counting the membership fee as part of the expense account would run this percentage up to "something like 14." In what way can the "national" system be made as economical to borrowers, in such circumstances, as the local, unless by showing that the "frozen out" members leave enough of their profits in the treasury to offset the big expense account? The organ of the "nationals" has in the last year conceded that the local system is the more economical. "The nationals cannot loan money," it said, "in competition with the locals where interest rates are equally high. Wherever the locals are able to supply the demand for money, the nationals will find their occupation gone." Some of the "nationals," seeing already that their promises of maturing shares cannot be kept, have introduced the feature of a "guaranty maturity fund." Of course the officers who contribute to such a fund see some way to recoup themselves for the outlay.

England has furnished some startling examples of the danger of "broadening" simple co-operative concerns, and departing from their legitimate fields. No country has demonstrated more satisfactorily than England the value of the building and loan system as a means of saving and a method of home acquiring. So perfectly had the system worked there through long years that the public came to place full confidence in any system that bore the attractive name. In this way vast associations have grown up there, with assets running into millions of pounds. With the growth of deposits came an enlargement of the business system, so that the big associations came to be really banks of deposit and discount. The Liberator, whose recent failure caused such wide-spread suffering, began by receiving deposits from members only. Then it advertised to pay from four to five per cent. on any deposits. With an accumulation of funds, and a necessity to keep them employed, came reckless lending. It stood behind a speculative contractor who put up enormous blocks of buildings in London which did not rent. When the contractor came to the end of his rope he found the building association in his company, and the crash followed. What has happened in England can just as easily happen here, and the result will not be prevented simply because in the list of officers may be found some honored names.

Building and Loan Associations have a value to any community aside from their pecuniary aspect, which is always recognized wherever they have been established.

Albert Shaw, Ph.D., in vol. i., No. 4, Publications of the American Economic Association, says:

"The success of the Building Societies in St. Paul is quite as complete, all things considered, as in the Pennsylvania cities. They have become an accepted local institution, destined to play a growingly important part in the building up of the city, and in the development of thrift and providence among wage-earners. . . . But even more important than their mere material achievements for the city, and for their members individually, has been their social and moral value, in counteracting the tendency of a city population to wider divergence between rich and poor, and to the development of a proletariat class. The typical American citizen is a free-holder, and has a home which is his castle. His independence and his virtue depend not a little upon his worldly condition. The Building Society is above all things to be commended as a conservator of the home and family institutions that underlie all our national greatness and power."

F. A. Richards, Bank Examiner in Maine, in a report for 1892 on the associations of that State, says:

"The key to the almost uniform success of Building and Loan Associations is to be found in the intimate relations which they hold to shareholders, and especially to borrowers. Not only do they make it possible for persons having but small incomes to build homes for themselves by loaning money on unfinished property, as the money is needed to advance the work, repayable in small instalments, but they exercise a scrupulous supervision over the interests of the borrower. The condition and situation of his property, the plans of the architect, the estimates, the character of the contractor, the building material, the work of the builder—all are carefully inspected by competent judges, and subject to their approval. The Building and Loan Association thus forms a supervisory board, whose assistance to the borrower is invaluable. . . . The educational character of these institutions is far from being one of their least important features."

Willis S. Paine, LL.D., Superintendent of the Banking Department of New York State, in the introduction to his work on the New York laws relating to Building Associations, says:

"These associations serve as a barrier against the dangerous paternalism urged on the State by men of questionable statesmanship, and they become likewise the foes of communism, creating habits of accumulation and assuring the privacy of homes. Such organizations become indirectly valuable moral agencies as a partial solution of the tenement-house problem, and hence are worthy of careful attention. The independent home secures removal from immoral tendencies, the adornment of domestic life, and full sway for the influence of wise training and good example. Whatever helps to remove the youth of the nation from the terrible and ever-present temptations of many of the crowded tenement-dens, from the accustomed debaucheries of drunken wretches in neighboring rooms, and from the shamelessness of those who oftentimes exist in them, works blessings for the peace and prosperity of the State. They are not a cure-all, however, but may, if loosely managed, prove a serious injury to the frugal and industrious wage-earners who invest in them."

The Chief of the New Jersey Bureau of Statistics of Labor and Industries said, in his Report for 1886:

"From the reports which have been forwarded to the Bureau these New Jersey associations are generally in a very prosperous condition, and a great benefit, not only to the individual members, but to the community at large; for they are increasing the number of tax-paying, property-owning citizens, and making it comparatively easy for an industrious working-man to own a home."

SOME PRACTICAL RESULTS OF BUILDING ASSOCIATIONS

"So manifold are the bearings of money upon the lives and characters of mankind, that an insight which should search out the life of a man in his pecuniary relations would penetrate into almost every cranny of his nature," says Henry Taylor. "He who knows, like St. Paul, both how to spare and how to abound, has great knowledge. For if we take account of all the virtues with which money is mixed up—honesty, justice, generosity, charity, frugality, forethought, self-sacrifice—and of their correlative vices, it is a knowledge which goes near to cover the length and breadth of humanity; and a right measure and manner of getting, saving, spending, giving, taking, lending, borrowing, and bequeathing, would almost argue a perfect man."

While the accumulation of wealth is mixed up with many of the grievous evils of this world, this statement of the importance of a right method of saving will not be denied; and of equal importance with a knowledge of saving is the knowledge how best to use what one has saved. The great initial problem with the multitude is how to save at all. Next comes the needed lesson, how not to squander what has been accumulated.

Experience has shown that some *system* is absolutely necessary to induce a large proportion of the persons of moderate means to lay aside a part of their incomes. The smaller the income, the greater, of course, is the temptation to spend it all in order to supply wished-for comforts of life. When money saving means a denial of some creature comfort, some equivalent for the denial must be presented clearly to view. The naturally frugal spy out this equivalent for themselves. But there are so many who are not by nature frugal; and it is for them that a *system* must be devised.

The most efficient system of this kind should combine three things: 1, An easily perceived inducement to save; 2, regularity in laying aside the savings; 3, as much compulsion as may be in enforcing the economy.

The most widely known system of this kind is that which is supplied by the savings banks. The value of these banks in our social economy is universally conceded. But, tested by the above requirements, it must be acknowledged that they are in part lacking. The satisfaction felt by the depositor in his growing deposit, and the knowledge of the value it will be to him in the future, supply the inducement. But as he may make his deposits at his own pleasure, and suffer no penalty if he stops them altogether, the second and third requisites named are wanting. Here another system—not so generally understood, but long tried and rapidly extending its operations —claims attention. This is the form of co-operation which I have

A Building and Loan Association receiving Monthly Dues.
(From an instantaneous photograph.)

just described as the Building and Loan Association. In view of the growing interest in the subject, and the eager demand that is manifested for the opinions of members who have tested these associations, as well as the experiments of different associations with particular plans of business, I propose to bring together some experiences, gathered by personal inquiry, and by correspondence with officers of associations all over the country. A sufficient demonstration of the importance of the subject will be found in the following statistics, compiled from the reports of 4,000 of these associations in the United States, and printed in a recent report of the Secretary of Internal Affairs of Pennsylvania:

Shares	5,450,000	Assets	$336,485,080
Members	872,000	Receipts, one year	139,323,934
Borrowers	272,000	Expenses	1,375,960
Borrowed shares	1,496,000	Gains	70,512,200

Important elements of the Building and Loan Association system are regular dates for making the payments and the infliction of a fine on delinquents. If a non-borrower is delinquent he knows that the fine will reduce his profits, and the borrower has the same inducement to be punctual, with the added knowledge that continued defaults will be followed by a foreclosure of his mortgage, and the consequent loss of his home. These are advantages which the Building and Loan Association system has over the savings bank. In addition it may be stated that the associations are conducted much more economically than the banks, that they consequently pay larger dividends, that they can be successfully carried on in places too small to support a bank, and that, by advancing money to members to purchase homes, they provide an immediate investment, and give the borrower the strongest possible inducement to continue his saving.

The State of Massachusetts has an excellent law governing these associations, and they have thrived there for many years without, I believe, a single failure. The Massachusetts law calls them Co-operative Banks, and it is very specific as to their business methods, leaving much less latitude to the by-laws than the statutes of other States do. The growth of the associations there has been especially rapid during the last year, twenty-seven new ones having been formed in that time. The number of members on October 31, 1889, was 36,747, and the assets amounted to $7,041,001. I have secured some very interesting statements of the experiences of Massachusetts members who have actually secured the ownership of homes through this system of co-operation.

J. T., a carpenter, owns the house in Wollaston, a suburb of Quincy, Mass., which is represented in the illustration below. Here is his story: "I have been connected with the Pioneer Co-operative Bank from its beginning. I took some of the very first shares, built a

House of a Carpenter at Wollaston, Mass., cost $1,800.

house, and finished paying for it last August. It has been a good thing for me. I could not have done as well in any other way. If I had borrowed the money of a savings bank I would have paid the interest, but not the principal. I had about $1,000 of my own to start with, and the loan of $700 I got enabled me to put up the house. It was eleven years ago last July that I borrowed the money. My monthly payment, including principal and interest, was $7.70. The house cost $1,800. Things were cheaper then than they are now. It would cost $2,100 to build the same house to-day. I have had a family of six children, so that there have been eight of us to support. We had no money coming in from any source except what I earned; the children were too small to earn anything. We had to live pretty close, but we did it, and now we have the house all paid for, so there is no longer any rent. I like the co-operative system well. I would always have been in debt if it had not been for the co-operative bank. The money cost me six per cent. I have had work right along in the same place for thirty-three years. I am now fifty-three years of age. A young man cannot do better than to try this system if he wants to get a home of his own. I am going to build again on the same plan. I shall borrow the money of the bank and build another house. The rent will pay the interest and all of the dues, and at the end of eleven years I shall own the house clear. The rent will cover the taxes and insurance, too. The house I now own has seven rooms, with city water."

Here is the story of another Massachusetts borrower, John J. F., a coachman, living at No. 39 Sawyer Street, Boston (Roxbury):

"It was eleven years ago, the twenty-second of January, 1890, that I bought nine shares of the co-operative bank. There was much building going on then, and I had to pay nine per cent. for my loan. But all stockholders have a privilege of buying the money over again, and I bought again and got it for seven and a half, after three years. It cost me about $20 to get my papers renewed. My monthly payments were $23.80 at first, but afterward they were $18.80. I bought the house and 904 feet of land for $1,900, paying $200 down. Inside of eleven years I held the place with a clear title. The house has eleven rooms, city water, and sewer connection. I have had but one child to support. I have had only $35 a month since I bought the house, and for the last six years I have had nothing to do for three months every summer. I did not have a cent coming to me outside my wages, and nobody gave me a cent to make my payments. But I had to work hard and save my money. I did not dress in expensive clothing and go like a dude on the streets with a cane. If a man does that he will never get anything done. I got the idea of saving and building from some other coachmen I met at Newport, from Philadelphia, who owned their own homes in this way.

"Now, I am rather fond of giving advice, and I would say to any laboring man who is industrious and wants a home for himself and his family—especially if he is a mechanic, or one who works by the day or month, or piece-work—get into some corporation like this. When they are paying their monthly dues they are really paying for their own houses."

It should be explained that this investor received his board from his employer, which permitted him to make his payments on the wages he received. His house is a small two-story brick one, with a mansard roof, standing at the end of a block. It is well built, neatly kept, and tastefully furnished.

Co-operation of this kind has been tested longer and more thoroughly in Pennsylvania than in any other of our States. As a consequence, many variations in the methods of transacting the associations' business have been introduced in different cities and towns, none of them, of course, in conflict with the co-operative principle. In Reading, where there are forty associations, the "terminating," or single series plan, is very popular. This plan is not so generally adopted throughout the country as the "serial," because in the latter the addition of new members from time to time at the starting price of the original stock keeps up the supply of borrowers. A "terminating" association, in time, requires a large payment to become a member (all the stock being kept at the same price), and it becomes difficult to find use for the funds. But many of the Reading co-operators, a large number of whom are wage-earners, and many of foreign birth, have always manifested a disposition to see one series of stock attain its par value before another is begun. All the terminating associations there are operated on practically the same principle, which may be thus described: The par value of shares is usually $200, $300, or $500, the most popular amount being $300 or $500. The monthly dues on the $200 shares are $1 per share, while on the others they are $2. An unusual feature is that there is a fixed premium demanded of both borrowers and non-borrowers; on a $300 share this is $30, and on a $500 share $50. In the first three years of an association's life, the competition of bidders for the money in the treasury

Row of Houses in Reading, Pa., built by Building and Loan Associations.

is generally so brisk that the premiums are run up to $5 a share above the fixed amount. After that, a borrower can generally get accommodation at the fixed rate, upon good security. The regular interest rate is six per cent. When the bidding for loans by members becomes slack, or falls off, as it does when an association has run five years or more, then the directors look out for other means of investment. Sometimes the money is loaned to other associations whose funds in hand do not satisfy their borrowers. A larger use, however, is found in buying lots of ground, and erecting buildings thereon, which are sold at prices varying from $2,000 to $7,000 each. The picture opposite shows a row of these houses. I am informed that a ready market is almost always found for them; if a season of hard times comes on, the associations are "easy" with the purchasers. I have said that non-borrowers also pay the fixed premium in these associations. To illustrate: Z invests in four $500 shares, paying in $8 a month as dues for eleven or twelve years, as the case may be. When the final distribution of assets is made he receives four times $500 ($2,000), less the fixed premium of $200.

The growth of Reading has been so assisted by the building and loan associations, that a few months ago, the Board of Trade there tried to induce them to lend out their funds to stimulate new business enterprises, particularly manufactures. Only one favorable response was received, however, to the proposition, wise conservatism having prevailed. A new association has since been started there, with a large amount of capital subscribed, whose constitution contains a special provision for loaning funds to manufactories. Innovations of this kind endanger the good reputation of the building and loan association system. They are mixed up with speculation, and are certain in time to incur disaster. When this system of co-operation has had its excellence and safety proved, its friends should insist that it be not endangered by speculative experiments. If co-operative manufacturing offers a field anywhere, let it be conducted under its own name.

Of the general results of co-operative home-winning in Reading, a resident of that city writes me: "Though building associations have been in continuous operation here over thirty years, the management of their business has been in such able and safe hands that only one has had a defaulting treasurer in all that period. The community, almost without exception, holds them in high esteem. When the Schiller Association terminated, it paid its stockholders twelve per cent. The Franklin expired in ten years, and its stockholders realized twelve per cent."

Another Pennsylvania city where this form of co-operation has stood the test of long trial is Pittsburg, its extensive industries furnishing a large population who can hope to become house owners in no other way. The picture below represents the house which a Pittsburg clerk owns by the aid of one of these associations. His

House of a Clerk in Pittsburg, Pa., cost about $2,200.

story shows how economically a business of this kind can be conducted, and how capable wage-earners are to manage it.

"When I had purchased my lot, I took twenty-two shares of building association stock. The par value in my association was $100. I was permitted to borrow $2,200 on my stock and lot. At our second meeting, as many slips of paper as there were stockholders, and numbered from one up, were put into a hat, and each man took out one.

The drawer of No. 1 was entitled to borrow the first money paid in. I got a big number, which would have prevented me from borrowing for about six years. Fortunately the man who drew No 2 was not in a hurry, and I exchanged with him. Every week I paid 30 cents a share principal, and 12 cents a share interest, a total of $9.24, a heavy drain on my pocketbook; but I kept it up until our stock reached par and the association expired, which happened after five years and six months. At the final settlement we found that $82 had been paid in dues on each share, the par of which was $100. So I made $18 on each share. I had paid in interest $732.16. To sum up my experience, I had been allowed to pay back the loan in such small weekly instalments as would not be accepted by a big corporation, and virtuallp I only paid $1.15 a week interest, or less than three per cent. I place the actual interest paid as the amount left after subtracting $396, the gain on the shares, from $732.16, the amount I was credited on my book as interest paid. I never could have secured a home in any other way, and I had the pleasure of living in my own house from the start.

" Our association was operated on economical principles. We met in a cigar store, paid no rent, and the only salaried officer was the secretary. The initiation fee of 25 cents a member, with the fines, paid the biggest part of our expenses. Before the association expired the stockholders had all become borrowers. A Pittsburg blacksmith, who is still working at his trade, and who has never earned over $3 a day, owns $75,000 of real estate, while a city official in Municipal Hall owns $30,000 worth, all secured by the aid of building and loan associations. As a general rule, these men bought improved property and made the rent pay both dues and interest."

New York is far behind not only Philadelphia, that great city of co-operative homes, but cities insignificant in size by comparison, as regards these associations. A principal reason for this is her insular situation, and the consequent lack of any suburban district of her own where land is within the reach of men of moderate means. The system, too, received a set back in New York State through mismanagement some years ago, from which it has been slow to recover. The reaction has begun, however, and a number of associations are doing good work in the city, although the majority of their loans are made on property outside the city limits. Some of these associations are in the hands of newspaper workers; one, with over a thousand members, is conducted by teachers in the public schools, with ladies in the board of directors, and one took the well-known name, "Western Union." The latter claims the honor of starting the renewal of interest in this subject in New York City after the long period of inactivity. The association was incorporated in January, 1885, after two years of preliminary effort on the part of a few New York telegraphers. The management is very conservative, all temptation to speculation by the association being prevented by a clause in the constitution which forbids it to buy property. During a period of five years it received and invested $153,000, loaned to ninety members, who are now in possession of their own homes, for which they are paying in easy instalments. It is conducted on the serial plan. It makes loans on accepted real estate anywhere within one hundred miles of the city, and it does not restrict its membership to telegraphers. I select this association for notice only in order to show that building and loan associations are a possibility even in a metropolis like New York.

As none of the series is old enough to have matured, none of the borrowers can be said strictly to "own" his home. But a good example is afforded of the satisfactory working of the system by the statement of Mr. F. A. C., the manager of the Western Union Telegraph Office in the Windsor Hotel. His house is in Mount Vernon, three miles outside the city limits. A view of it is given in the illustration opposite. "I had in 1885," said Mr. C., "a lot valued at $700. In March, 1885, I borrowed of the association $2,000, and in March, 1886, I borrowed $200 more, which completed my house. Since the last date my monthly payments have been: dues, $11; interest, $11; premium, $4.35; a total of $26.35. Since the house was built I have added the corner lot to my plot, and I now value the house and lot at $3,370. My house would easily rent for $30 a month, which is more than all my monthly payments."

House of a Western Union Telegraph Superintendent at Mount Vernon, N. Y., cost $2,200, exclusive of ground.

If this borrower's association closes out his series in nine years, his interest account will stand as follows:

Total payments per year ($26.35 a month)	$316 20
In nine years	2,845 80
Interest charge (deducting $2,200 principal)	645 80
Interest charge per year	71 76

which is at the rate of but a little over three per cent. a year.

Brooklyn, N. Y., has a large extent of adjoining unimproved property, not held at exorbitant prices, and it is therefore a good field for co-operative building. The latest list of associations there numbers twenty-nine.

The illustration below represents one of the houses acquired by the members of a Brooklyn association. It is in Sixty-seventh

House in Sixty-seventh Street, Bay Ridge, L. I., cost $2,500.

Street, Bay Ridge, within five blocks of the Brooklyn boundary. It measures 20 × 30 feet, with an extension, two stories, and attic; has a parlor, dining-room, and kitchen on the first floor, three bedrooms and bath-room on the second, and three finished rooms in the attic. It is built in the best manner, with furnace, range, hot and cold water, and gas, and it cost $2,500. The owner borrowed $2,400, and his monthly payments, including interest, premium, and dues are $30. His balance sheet stands thus:

Former annual payment for rent..................		$420 00
Payments to association........................	$360 00	
Taxes (less than)..............................	20 00	
Insurance	7 50	
Extra car fare now required....................	20 00	
Total......................................		$407 50
Allow four per cent. interest on owner's equity in premises ($600)............................		24 00
Grand total...............................		$431 50

or $11.50 a year more than he expended as a rent-payer. The present estimate is that the interest rate of this association's borrowers, when their stock matures, will be about five and a half per cent.

Here is a further illustration: "A teacher in one of the public schools in Brooklyn borrowed $4,000 of the association, and built a three-story apartment-house, with all modern improvements. She was paying $25 a month rent for a flat when she built. She now occupies a flat in her own building, and rents the remaining two for $25 and $24, respectively. Her account stands thus:

Mortgage...	$4,000 00
Equity	3,000 00
Payments to association per annum	$600 00
Taxes	100 00
Insurance..	6 00
Interest (four per cent.) on equity..................	120 00
Total...	$826 00
Deduct rentals received	588 00
Leaves her net rent.................................	238 00

or at the monthly rate of $19.84, while all the time she is paying off her debt."

The illustration below shows at a glance what a poor man who lives in rented apartments may gain by building a house of his own through the co-operative system. Mr. H. is a man of family, in the employ of a New York business firm. He rented four rooms in a building on a business street in Hackensack, N. J., paying $9 a month rent. The lower floor was used for business purposes. His apartments were crowded and inconvenient, and by no means safe

"Then and Now." Four rooms rented in the upper floor of this building at $9 per month.

in case of fire. In the spring of 1888, he bought three lots near the town, where some farm land had been recently cut up into building lots, paying $75 each. Then he borrowed $1,100 of the Hackensack Building and Loan Association, on

House built and occupied by the same man in Hackensack, N. J., cost $1,050, monthly payment $11.50.

the three lots, and put up his house, at a cost of $1,050, the association lending him very close because of the smallness of the loan, the certain rise in the value of his property, and his excellent character. His premium (gross) was $38.50. Now he pays to the association, as dues and interest, only $11.50 a month—which is only $2.50 a month more than he paid as rent—and in about eleven years from the start he will have the premises free and clear. Meanwhile, he has a house all to himself. And a very neat and attractive house it is, although it cost so little, with a parlor, a dining-room, and a kitchen on the first floor, and three bedrooms above. His wife said to me when they were settled: "It came very hard to pay out that $9 a month for rent, but now we know the money we pay to the association is paying for our home."

An association which has had a remarkable history is the Mutual No. 1, of Bayonne, N. J. (a suburb of Jersey City). It was organized on the terminating plan, in June, 1879, and its final statement was dated August 12, 1889. The original estimate was that its stock would mature in ten years. It actually matured in one hundred and twenty-three months. The secretary's final report says: "Loans since 1885 had to be made outside the association, mostly on call, realizing whatever interest could be obtained, and only while the money was employed. The serial plan has a decided advantage in this respect; the introduction of new series provides employment for money, and prevents accumulation. . . . Membership, whether investors or borrowers, was not confined to any class of society; professional persons, merchants, wage-earners of all degrees, and others of independent means, men and women, shared in the prosperity. The officers of the association, except the secretary and treasurer (one person), served without compensation or emolument of any kind. No one ever lost a cent by any act of the association. The association never lost a cent of dues, interest, or fines; never foreclosed a mortgage, never had a fire insurance case to settle, and never owned an inch of real estate."

The picture on p. 202 represents one of the homes bought through this association. I give it to show that it is not only wage-earners who may be benefited by this form of co-operation. This house is owned and occupied by a wholesale dry-goods merchant, doing business in this city, or, to be exact, by his wife, as he deeded it to her. "I went to Bayonne to live," said this gentleman, "about the time the

House of a Wholesale Dry-Goods Merchant at Bayonne, N. J.

association was started. A friend mentioned the enterprise to me, and I took five shares to see what it amounted to. Soon I bought some lots and decided to build. As I did not care to take the money for the house out of my business, I borrowed it from the association after taking more shares. My dues and interest were $40 a month, and my payments ceased in ten years and two months. My experience was altogether satisfactory, and I would recommend the same course to any man in my position, who does not feel like taking out of his business the money to buy or build a home."

Some associations in Jersey City, N. J., have found it advisable to erect buildings to serve as their headquarters. The picture opposite represents one of these, the building of the Columbia Association. The reasons which induced the erection of this building were as follows: The association was organized in the outskirts of the city, and in the heart of a district which, after being occupied for farm purposes, had recently been cut up into lots. A change of ownership in the building where the association met having compelled it to seek new quarters, the proposal was made to erect a building of its own, which took definite shape. The necessary money was taken from the general funds. The building complete, with lot, cost $4,730.65. It was occupied in August, 1888. In the first fourteen months it brought in a net revenue of $346.14, which was a little over six per cent. on the investment. The ground floor is used as a hall, with a real estate office in front. The upper floor contains six large rooms, with bath and all other modern improvements. Arrangements have been made to rent the hall, which will increase the income.

As the association is a serial one, and the building will be a per-

Hall built by the Columbia Association, Jersey City, cost, with lot, $4,730.

manent asset, as each series matures the value of the building will be estimated, and a settlement be made with the retiring shareholders on that basis, as would be done in a business firm on the retirement of a partner. It is probable that the association will eventually realize a handsome profit on the investment.

An association with a very interesting history, to which I would be glad to devote more space than I can command, is the Mutual of Newark, N. J. This association was organized in June, 1867, and is still in prosperous operation. I can call attention only to two points in regard to it. The period of its existence covers the panic and the hard times of the '70s. Although, up to 1877, it had loaned in Essex County (a manufacturing district) $156,800, it had been obliged to foreclose on only three pieces of property. During the latter part of 1877 and in 1878, twelve pieces of property came into possession of the association, on some of which losses were made. There has been no foreclosure in the last eleven years. It received from 1867 to 1889, cash, from all sources, $659,603.61; has lent on bond and mortgage $443,925; has collected $5,501.43 in fines, and $105,376.86 as interest; and its total expenses for twenty-two years were only $11,483.25. It has always been conducted on the "gross" premium plan. A second point worth noting is the long terms of its officers. On the publication of its history in pamphlet form, in 1886, the president had held his office for ten years (after three years as vice-president, and four as director); the treasurer for nineteen years; and the secretary, Mr. John Pardue, for sixteen years, after three years as director. The same treasurer and secretary are still in office.

Building and loan associations flourished in Central and Western New York during the period when the movement was at a standstill in the Southeastern part of the State. The picture opposite shows the house of a young business man in Rochester. He figures as follows on his investment: "My total payments to the association are $7.25 each week. If the association pays annual dividends of an average of ten per cent., as, from its record, there is every reason to believe it will do, my mortgage will be paid off in a little less than nine years, and I shall have paid but 3.95 per cent. interest for the use of the money."

Building and loan associations have been in operation in St. Paul, Minn., for over twenty years, and nowhere have they vindicated their object more conclusively than in that city and its twin, Minneapolis. The illustration on p. 206 is the picture of the house (in its winter

House of a Young Business Man in Rochester, N. Y. Built on a weekly payment of $7.25, for a period of about nine years.

dress) of D. H., a tailor, at No. 183 E. Belvidere Street, St. Paul. Here is his own story of the way in which he acquired it:

"I was induced to join a building association in 1876, when I began by saving $10 a month. I was in several series at different times, but it seemed that, as often as I got a few hundred dollars ahead, I would have to use it to meet some pressing need. But I always began over again, until in March, 1883, having about $350 to my credit, I thought I would 'plant it' where I couldn't get it out so easily. So I bought two lots for $700 and paid $350 cash on them. In about a year and a half I had paid off the mortgage and a street assessment.

Times were rather flush in 1885, and I bought thirteen shares of stock of the St. Paul B. and L. Association No. 1, for about $375. I had been paying rent for years (I am over fifty now), at from $20 to $25 a month. I now found that I could borrow enough money of the association on my lots (which had increased in value to $1,500) and stock

House of a Tailor in St. Paul, Minn., cost $1,860.

to build a good house, and have only $26 a month to pay on it. I got $1,860 net, of the association, with which I put up an eight-room house, two stories high. I have as fine a view as any of the nabobs of Summit Avenue, and can see up the river half-way to Minneapolis.

"I shall have to pay for thirty-one months more, at $26 a month, when I will be out of debt, and own a place worth $4,000. I have refused an offer of $3,000 for the house and one lot."

I am indebted to Mr. Thomas A. Rice, of St. Louis, author of a useful work on building association book-keeping, for the following account of the growth of this system of co-operation in his city, coupled with his own personal experience:

"I joined my first building association, the Hibernia, at its organization, in July, 1873; I was totally in the dark as to its methods, but I took some shares on the advice of friends. Some three years later, on the resignation of the secretary, being a practical accountant, I was put in his place, and was thus forced to study the subject in all its bearings. I now say, unhesitatingly, that there is nothing on the face of the earth so beneficial to all who join it—especially to wage-earners who need help and encouragement in saving their money and getting a home, as a well-managed building association.

"The six associations of which I am now secretary have loaned out $891,200 to two hundred and ninety-two borrowers, the majority of whom used the money for building houses. When the Hibernia was about five years old I, myself, borrowed $2,500 on my five shares and bought a house and lot, living there for ten years, and now renting it for $25 a month. Of course, since the association matured (in 1882, having run just nine years), I have had nothing to pay on it. A year and a half before the Hibernia matured it retired all its free shares, paying the stockholders the full amount of money paid in by them, and interest on the same at the rate of seventeen per cent. per annum for the average time.

"Seeing the success of this association, I easily persuaded its members, and some other persons, to organize the Laclede Association, now eight and a half years old. Of this association I was secretary for the first two years, and I still hold fifty-five shares of its stock. On these I borrowed $11,000, and bought a five-story stone front building, No. 322 Chestnut Street. My monthly dues and interest on this loan are $110, and I receive $125 a month rent. I spent some $2,000 of my own money on it.

"When the Hibernia, whose capital was $250,000, divided into

House of a Building and Loan Association Secretary in St. Louis, cost, without lot, $7,000.

five hundred shares of $500 each, matured in 1882, the members were so well pleased that the Hibernia No. 2 was organized the same day, with a capital of $500,000, divided into $200 shares. Every share of this stock was taken at the first meeting, and the stock sold the next day at a premium of fifty per cent. To accommodate those who could not get into this association, I organized the Mound City six months later, with a capital of $600,000 divided into $300 shares. This association, during the last seven years, has handled $511,742.50, at a total expense of $6,221.82—or only one and a quarter cent on every dollar. To-day we have in St. Louis about one hundred and ten associations, of an average capital of $600,000, and a total membership of about forty thousand.

"In May, 1886, I borrowed from the Mound City Association $11-100, with which I purchased a lot at Garfield and Spring Avenues, and put up the house shown in the picture opposite, $7,000 of the money was used to erect the house. My monthly payments on this loan are $129.50, $2 dues on each of thirty-seven shares, and $55.50 interest. This is pretty heavy, but my lot is 141 × 120, paid for out of this loan, and the vacant part has advanced in value to about $5,000."

Cincinnati supports about four hundred building associations, with an average capital of about $2,000,000. In the twenty years of their

House of a Cincinnati Bookkeeper, cost, with lot, $2,400.

history there, not half a dozen of those properly organized have met with disaster, and in no case has there been a total failure. At least ten thousand houses, mostly in the suburbs, have been paid for through the associations, their average cost being about $3,500. The picture on p. 209 shows one of these suburban houses, owned by the bookkeeper of a Cincinnati firm. He took two shares, worth at par $500 each. The weekly dues are $2; his weekly interest on $1,000 borrowed is $1.20, and his weekly premium 16 cents, making an annual payment of $174.72, which is about what he paid for rent before building. It is calculated that his shares will mature in less than eight years. The house and lot cost $2,400.

The associations have found a secure hold in the Far West—in Utah, California, and Oregon. The picture below shows the pretty home of one of the members of the Citizens' Building and Loan

House of a Bookkeeper at Berkeley, a suburb of San Francisco, Cal., cost $2,000.

Association of San Francisco, Cal., at Berkeley, just across the bay. The owner, a bookkeeper, borrowed $2,000, and had his mortgage cancelled in one hundred and eleven months.

While, for some reason, savings institutions have not gained so general a foothold in our Southern States as they have in the North,

House of a Government Clerk in Washington, D. C., cost $4,000.

the building association system is doing an excellent work in many Southern cities. I have space to speak of their work in only three of these cities, but this may be looked upon as typical.

There are a number of associations in Washington, D. C., the Equitable being, perhaps, the most prominent. It has about four thousand members, at least ninety-five per cent. of whom are clerks in the Government departments, clerks in stores, small merchants, and wage-earners. Some five hundred are colored people, and probably thirty-three per cent. are females. The loans have ranged from $100 to $8,000. There have been eighteen issues of stock, embracing 42,623 shares, of which 28,213 have been redeemed. The association has made about one thousand nine hundred loans, has foreclosed on only one, and has never lost a dollar.

The illustration on p. 211 represents the house of one of the members of this association, a clerk in the Surgeon-General's office. It is situated on "Mt. Pleasant," a northern suburb of the city. It was built two years ago at a cost of $4,000, with money borrowed of the association.

The building and loan (or "homestead associations," as they are locally called in some instances) are a recognized feature among the business institutions of New Orleans, and a considerable part of the annual "trade editions" of the *Picayune* and the *Times-Democrat* are devoted to them. There are fifteen associations in the city, and six or eight in other parts of Louisiana. The *Times-Democrat*, in its trade edition of September, 1888, said: "All of those in the city are in excellent financial condition, and hundreds of homes have been secured for members. The solidity of these organizations is demonstrated by the fact that, while several of them have gone out of business during the year, or consolidated with other associations owing to lack of membership, not a single shareholder has lost a nickel. While the number of residences has been materially increased, the number of renters has been proportionately diminished, and landlords have been compelled to pay more attention to the comfort of their tenants."

A representative Southern home, secured by co-operation, is shown in the picture opposite, the house of Mr. P. K., a pressman on the *Picayune*. It is situated at No. 81 Bolivar Street. Mr. K. has held his present position since 1886. When the People's Homestead Association was organized in New Orleans, the business manager of the *Picayune* advised the employees to join it. Mr. K. subscribed for eight shares, and a few years later took twenty more. He had been a rent-payer since 1866, but his savings in the association now enabled him to enjoy the independence of a home of his own. He paid $3,400 for his house and lot, and has land enough to set off another building lot if he were inclined. By the time he has paid in full for the property, his outlay, including taxes and insurance, will amount to $4,227.50. The place is said to have cost originally over $12,000.

House of a Pressman in New Orleans, cost, with Lot, $4,227.

Atlanta, Ga., has enjoyed the benefits of these associations for a number of years, and the members there have given some interesting testimony to the benefits they have received. The secretary of the People's Mutual Loan and Building Association sent out postal-cards to all the members, a few years ago, asking them to give him a statement of their experience. Here are a few of the answers:

"The association has been the means of my saving $1,600."

"The association has kept our boys' money safely invested, and they are $925 better off than two years ago." (These boys had formerly spent all their money for drink.)

"I owe all I have in the world to the association."

The secretary of this association, Mr. E. P. McBurney, writes to me: "A negro who, when he joined, had but $500, has built a store costing $4,500 in which he does business, and he is worth $6,000. The rent of half the building more than pays his dues. Another negro member has built the house in which he lives through the association. A mechanic told me the other day that he had for four years been increasing his holding of stock, until he now paid in $30 a month, whereas, four years ago, he did not think he could save a cent."

If this testimony to the beneficial operations of co-operative building and loan associations, gathered from so wide a territory, seems one-sided, I have only to say that in all the correspondence I have had on the subject I have not received one complaint. But the testimony should be accepted as proving, not that the system is not open to abuses and losses under bad management, but that beyond dispute it is one of the greatest means for the encouragement of thrift that man has devised. No method has ever been invented, in public or private affairs, to render the custody of funds entirely safe. But no investment and management can nearer approach safety than that of a mutual building and loan association, in which the officers are well chosen and in which *all* do their duty.

THE END.

www.ingramcontent.com/pod-product-compliance
Lightning Source LLC
Chambersburg PA
CBHW021834230426
43669CB00008B/966